C000151304

FALLING
into the
LIGHT

FALLING
into the
LIGHT

M.J. Wiley

atmosphere press

Copyright © 2021 M.J. Wiley

Published by Atmosphere Press

Cover design by Nick Courtright

Cover image: Courtesy of National Gallery of Art,
Washington

No part of this book may be reproduced
except in brief quotations and in reviews
without permission from the author.

Falling into the Light is a work of fiction.
While the story may be based on historical figures,
places, and events, the book should not be read
as a factual representation of history.

Falling into the Light
2021, M.J. Wiley

atmospherepress.com

PROLOGUE

Originating in India over 2,500 years ago, Buddhism was founded by Siddhartha Gautama, the privileged son of wealth and nobility. As a young adult, Gautama became obsessed with the world's suffering and abandoned his royal destiny so that he could dedicate his life to understanding and overcoming suffering through wisdom, morality, and mindfulness training. After attaining spiritual enlightenment under a Bodhi tree, Gautama became a Buddha and spent the remainder of his life sharing his experiences and teaching his followers about the spiritual path to Nirvana.

Under the formalization of the Tibetan Buddhist teachings, the most supreme monks, known as High Lamas, are dedicated to ensuring the continuity of the religion. The highest of these monks is the Dalai Lama, who is believed to be the reincarnated succession of Buddhist leaders throughout history. With the death of each Dalai Lama, the High Lamas are responsible for seeking out their next incarnated spiritual leader. The process of discovering this "spiritual being" entails probing the countryside guided by divine visions while scrutinizing spiritually precocious young boys in the remote villages of Tibet.

When the new Dalai Lama has been found and confirmed by the High Lamas, he is taken along with his family back to Lhasa and introduced as the new spiritual and secular leader of the Tibetan people. He then begins a rigorous religious training and monastic discipline until the age of eighteen, when he ascends to full power as His Holiness the Dalai Lama.

CHAPTER ONE

As a new day dawned over the sacred city of Lhasa, one could not help but feel the spiritual transcendence brought to light by the morning sun as it ascended above the freezing fog to illuminate towering mountains against a brilliant blue sky. Often referred to as the "roof of the world," the Tibetan Plateau was a vast highland sitting above 14,000 feet elevation. Surrounded by some of the highest mountains in the world, this region was home to pastoral nomads who thrived in extreme weather and isolation while raising livestock on the open grasslands. Nestled into these majestic mountains sat the Potala Palace, a virtual sanctuary in the sky. Built in the seventh century as the primary residence for the Dalai Lama and a spiritual center for the Buddhist cultures throughout Asia, the fortress-like palace rose thirteen stories and was crowned with gold, diamonds, pearls, and other precious gems to honor the sacred Buddhist saints of the past. At its pinnacle, the Potala complex served as residence, school, monastery, temple, and workplace to over 25,000

Tibetans every day.

It was 5 a.m. and the palace was already bustling with activity. It was traditional for Buddhist monks to rise before the sun so they could sit in quiet meditation before the day started in earnest. After completing his morning meditation, His Holiness the Dalai Lama walked down a massive hallway laden with historic murals, ancient scrolls and sculptures to a private deck overlooking the vast plateau framed by distant mountain ranges, where he spent the next hour exercising full-body prostrations in the brisk morning air while listening to the collective chants and prayer bells from the resident monks gathered in the temple below.

Following his daily meditation and exercises, the Dalai Lama returned to his private quarters to wash his body and shave both his face and head as a symbol of selfless humility and a denouncement of all worldly attachments. He then dressed in a simple saffron robe, wrapped several times around his lean and fit body, and sat down at a small table in the corner of his room to enjoy a simple breakfast of porridge, bread, and tea.

A slight knock on the door was answered by two servants pushing open the large heavy doors leading to the private chamber of the Dalai Lama, where he was now fully dressed and prepared for the events of the day.

"Good morning Your Holiness," said Panchen Lama casually in the Tibetan language as he entered the room and removed a folder from his shoulder bag. "I'd like to review your lecture notes once more."

Panchen Lama was the most senior lama in the monastery and the second-highest spiritual leader in Tibet, behind the Dalai Lama. It was Panchen Lama who led the search for the newly incarnated Dalai Lama in 1841, and it was he who took complete responsibility for the growth and development of His Holiness for the past twenty years.

"Yes, of course, Panchen," replied the Dalai Lama.

"There will be attendants from the Qing commission most certainly," said Panchen. "I am not concerned about any interference with your teachings, but we must not provoke them either."

"So, probably best not to mention the British Empire?" remarked the Dalai Lama with a slight grin on his face.

"Precisely," replied Panchen, choosing not to acknowledge the attempted humor. "Just stay aligned to your sermon, and you will be fine."

Panchen sat down at the table next to the Dalai Lama and opened his folder to review the notes further before they both proceeded to the lecture event.

As the Dalai Lama stood backstage at the Potala amphitheater, he could hear a low rumble coming from out front. The crowd was anxiously waiting for His Holiness to enter onto the stage for his monthly sermon and exchange with the Buddhist community. The Dalai

Lama was also anxious, as this was one of his favorite events, where he engaged in conversation and discourse with the common Buddhists from Lhasa, as well as the monks, students, and daily workers who took residency on the palace grounds.

Without delay, His Holiness pulled back the cloth screen at the side of the stage and walked gracefully onto the large empty platform. Suddenly, like a human tidal wave, the massive crowd fell silent and dropped to their knees and then into a full bow onto the ground. The wave of collapsing worshippers flowed toward the back for several seconds until the entire congregation had fallen into full reverence for their spiritual leader. In complete silence, the Dalai Lama proceeded to the front of the stage and assumed a lotus position on a small cushion. The amphitheater remained quiet for several minutes until the silence was broken by a harmonic chime, followed by the Dalai Lama warmly greeting his disciples and delivering a 30-minute discourse on the 'Hindrances Encountered on the Spiritual Path.' The sermon was followed by a performance from a small choir. The congregation was then led through a silent meditation before being gratefully thanked and blessed once more by the Dalai Lama.

Following the sermon, it was customary for the Dalai Lama to accept greetings and questions from the fellowship. His Holiness had taken a seat on one of the steps leading off-stage as a small crowd formed around him in front of the stage. One by one, the devotees approached the Dalai Lama and presented him with a ceremonial white scarf, which he then blessed both the scarf and his devoted worshipper.

On occasion, one of the followers would ask for a special blessing of a loved one, or for guidance through a difficult period or situation. His Holiness was more than happy to engage in these dialogues, as it usually brought joy and discovery to him, as well as his disciples.

As the crowd began to thin out, a woman approached the Dalai Lama, bowed in reverence, and handed him her white khata. The Dalai Lama took the scarf offering, kissed it, and lifted it over his head to be blessed by the heavenly spirits. As he did, he looked closer at the woman. She was wearing a simple dress with a scarf covering her head. Her pale face appeared lifeless with dark shadows engulfing her distant eyes. There was a moment of eye contact, where the Dalai Lama could see the grief and pain weighing heavily on her frail body. She lowered her head, averting her eyes from His Holiness before speaking.

"I am in deep suffering Your Holiness and desperately seek your guidance through this horrible nightmare," she said softly yet bluntly.

The Dalai Lama lowered the scarf into his lap, released his posture, leaned forward slightly, and whispered to the solemn soul in front of him. "I am overcome by the pain in your heart," he said. "Please, tell me what you will about this nightmare."

"I have lost my child to a miscarriage," the woman wept. "And my husband blames me for the loss and has left me." She barely completed her words before choking into tears.

The Dalai Lama sat speechless in front of the grieving woman. The extended silence created a womb of comfort between the two of them while insulating them from everyone else. His Holiness reached out and wrapped the khata over the shoulders of the crying woman. He then pulled her gently into his open arms and she collapsed into his mournful heart. The Dalai Lama held the woman for some time before responding.

"In a time like this, I feel words cannot hold a meaningful solution," His Holiness whispered as he leaned down and looked directly into the woman's grieving eyes. "Perhaps resting in quiet contemplation while accepting the truth that this was a very unfortunate event of which no one is to blame will give you the strength to persevere through this difficult time in your otherwise beautiful and blessed life."

After another moment of warm silence, the woman rose back to her feet, dried her tears with the white scarf, bowed politely to His Holiness, turned, and walked away, leaving the Dalai Lama alone on the empty stage.

Dressed in an old, worn monk's robe and a wide-brimmed straw hat, the Dalai Lama immersed himself in weeding and pruning one of the many elaborate and colorful palace gardens when Panchen found him.

"I've been looking all over for you, Your Holiness," Panchen said as he entered the garden and sat on a bench at the end of the row near the Dalai Lama.

"I'm sorry Panchen, I did not feel like being inside today," the Dalai Lama said with a tone of despair. "And working in the garden allows my mind to settle."

Panchen recognized the anguish in his progeny. "What's on your mind, son?" Panchen asked sincerely with his undivided attention.

The Dalai Lama paused before replying. "It's the woman at the end of the lecture yesterday," he said. "I don't think I helped her at all. I was at a loss for words."

"I thought you handled that very well," Panchen noted with certainty. "Words were not what that woman was seeking."

"Maybe, but the pain she felt deep inside was something greater than anything I have ever felt," the Dalai Lama said as he shook his head and gazed over the distant peaks, feeling small and incompetent.

"Listen to me, Gyatso," Panchen whispered with intention. "Nobody expects the Dalai Lama to have experienced every form of suffering to help them be happy. You are the chosen one, the reincarnated life force of every Buddhist saint over the past 2,500 years. Your wisdom comes from all of those who came before you. The people of Tibet see you as a symbol of the path to grace and happiness, not the answer to everyone's problems,"

Panchen finished and waited for a response.

When no response came, Panchen Lama stood up and started back toward the complex.

"Guru!" hollered the Dalai Lama from across the garden.

Panchen paused as His Holiness walked toward him through the garden. From the row of flowers next to Panchen, His Holiness reached over and presented his mentor with a beautiful yellow rose in full bloom.

"Thank you, Panchen," Gyatso yielded with a bow. "You know, it is said that the yellow rose is a symbol of friendship and caring."

Panchen accepted the rose. "When you are done playing in the dirt, we need to talk about the trip to Shanghai," he said with a gentle smile as he turned and walked away.

CHAPTER TWO

The Dalai Lama retired to his private chamber following a light dinner and tea. He was reading some scriptures while lying in bed when he heard a noise outside. He knew immediately that it was a pebble tapping against his window, and knew that it must be Lobsang, his childhood friend and confidant. He walked over and opened the window quietly.

"Gyatso!" whispered Lobsang. "Come with me into town. There is music on the square tonight!"

The Dalai Lama thought for a moment, then replied, "Yes, I will come! Meet me behind the stables after dark."

The Dalai Lama closed the window and went to his closet to dress. He grabbed the old monk's robe he wore when he was a youth in school. Everyone in school knew he was the Dalai Lama, but wearing similar clothes as the rest of the students seemed to make the kids and himself more at ease. He then slipped on the straw hat he wore in the garden and pulled it tight over his eyes. This would be enough to disguise his identity in town if he stayed in the background and did not draw attention to himself. When the sun was fully set, he proceeded out onto his private deck and climbed down the lattice before scrambling across the compound to the riding stables, where he met up with Lobsang.

Lobsang was a devout monastic who also grew up in the Potala palace. As the son of a married Lama working at one of the monasteries, Lobsang was accepted into the Potala school system and eventually into the monk training program offered to a select group of students. Lobsang and Gyatso first met as young children in the martial arts dojo. Learning martial arts was a compulsory discipline for all school-aged boys. One day Lobsang got somewhat carried away during a simulated attack exercise, and Gyatso ended up with a bloody nose. Needless to say, there was a mild panic by the teachers that day, but when Gyatso and Lobsang both fell onto the mats in laughter, calm was soon restored. The two young students quickly became friends for life and spent countless hours together growing up in the Potala palace.

The narrow streets of Lhasa's town square were lined on both sides with a stream of colorful fabric tents filled with handmade crafts, clothes, toys, food and most anything else that one could need or want. Prayer flags were strung from corner to corner, dimly lit by candle lights hanging overhead in the vendor tents. The evening was alive with crowds of people who came for shopping, socializing and entertainment every weekend at the square. Gyatso and Lobsang made their way to the far end of the square, where a Buddhist monument had been converted into a temporary stage for a band of monks harmonizing their drums, horns, and voices in joyful song. The two friends sat on a grassy hill behind the stage and listened to the music while watching the crowd mingle in the square. The atmosphere was casual, festive, and friendly, and it was exactly what the Dalai Lama needed.

Walking back up the steep hill to the palace grounds was never as much fun as running down the hill into town. The two friends paced themselves slowly as they talked.

"I met a missionary from America in town last week," said Lobsang.

"Really?" replied Gyatso. "Did he convert you into a Christian?"

"No, but he sure tried," Lobsang said, catching his breath. "If I understood more English, he might have succeeded!"

They both laughed, then continued up the hill in silence, no doubt thinking about the same thing.

"Have you ever wondered what it must be like in America?" Lobsang finally asked.

"Panchen says you can own one hundred hectares of land for free just by settling there and building a homestead," Gyatso replied.

"I've heard the land is warm and fertile with raging rivers too wide to cross," Lobsang said with childlike envy.

"Maybe so," Gyatso noted, "But Panchen also says the frontier is lawless and the natives are being overrun by immigrants."

"Perhaps, but it all sounds so exciting!" exclaimed Lobsang.

The young men continued their casual conversation as they proceeded up the hill to the palace. They soon reached the riding stables where they began their evening. They smiled, hugged, and bowed, before parting ways back to their private living quarters.

CHAPTER THREE

A team of servants shuttled back and forth from the palace kitchen while the High Lamas assembled around a large rectangular solid wood dining table draped in a formal tablecloth and an elaborate table runner full of assorted designs and colors. The palace dining room was staged with massive candle chandeliers hung from the high ceilings. A large granite fireplace burned warmly in the corner as the north-facing wall of windows, extending from the floor to the ceiling, revealed the rugged snowcapped peaks in the background.

The lunch was cleared, and tea was served when His Holiness stood to speak.

"Thank you all once again for coming together as we plan our journey to Shanghai," he said. "As you all know, we have been invited to participate in a leadership summit with China and some of our neighboring countries. We have been informed the summit is general and will cover several topics relevant to South Asia. However, according to the Chinese commission, the issues related to the growth and influence of foreign immigration on the region are of paramount importance," the Dalai Lama said as he glanced at his notes on the table.

The High Lamas considered the pause by His Holiness as an opportunity to comment amongst themselves in private. The low rumble of whispers soon grew into a roar of competing voices.

"Gentlemen, please!" said the Dalai Lama firmly as he raised a hand into the air. "We will all get a chance to speak. So please be respectful of your peers."

"Your Holiness," said Panchen Lama. "If I may begin with some background context. Given the recent occupation and subsequent cession of Hong Kong to the British Crown, the concerns of the Qing Dynasty are certainly justified. We can all assume this is only the beginning of the British expansion into Central China. However, it is also a fact that the Qing Dynasty is gaining in population and power and has pushed aggressively to expand their quest for land, food, and natural resources throughout Asia. We cannot assume that China is still aligned with the Tibetan interests and our continued sovereignty."

"Yes! Yes!" exclaimed another High Lama. "And what about the opium epidemic that has so devastated the coastal region! It was the British who brought opium into China as a currency for trade. And now it is ripping the souls out of the Chinese people."

With that, the rumble of voices rose to a roar again.

The Dalai Lama paused to let the Lamas vent their emotions. After the tension had been sufficiently released in the room and the teacups were all refilled by the servants, the Dalai Lama restarted the conversation.

"Now that we have a premise for the upcoming summit, I would like to discuss the position of the Tibetan people and the response we should have to any threats that may come out of this summit," His Holiness said as tactfully as he could, knowing the explosiveness of the room.

"Our position must be defensive. And our response must be stern and forceful," Panchen Lama declared to the room.

The Dalai Lama paused again, expecting another roar of conviction, but instead the room fell silent. The lamas quickly looked at Panchen Lama and then over to His Holiness for a reaction. Their eyes were alert with fear. Their faces flushed and pale as if the oxygen had just been drained from the room. Though he didn't show it, His Holiness was shocked by the stark reply as well. Tibet had always been a nation of neutrality, believing that a civil environment of peace and spiritual strength would always return in kind, protecting their community from outside influence and aggression. Furthermore, Tibetans had been so geographically isolated from the world that they never saw a need for military protection and therefore had no real means to engage in defense against another country's aggressions.

The room remained silent for some time, as they patiently waited for the Dalai Lama's response.

"While it is not in our nature to be aggressive and forceful," the Dalai Lama finally responded. "I have no doubt that Panchen Lama is well informed and has thoughtfully considered the situation we may find ourselves facing."

"Let me be clear," exclaimed Panchen Lama. "I am not promoting any form of aggressiveness or harmful violence. But I am suggesting that we need to prepare ourselves for oppressive behavior from both within China and abroad," Panchen stated. "There is a great political and economic gain to be had from territorial expansion, and some countries will stop at nothing to achieve their expansionist goals."

The mood of the room became guarded and somber. The lamas had never been exposed to such aggressive intentions from the outside and therefore had no response to offer as a legitimate proposal. The Dalai Lama continued to kindle the conversation as best he could, and Panchen Lama provided some valuable direction on collaborating with other governments in Central China. But the shocking volatility of the subject matter had depleted the energy from the High Lamas, and the meeting was soon adjourned.

After the High Lamas had left the meeting, Panchen refilled two cups of tea, walked over to the stone fireplace, and sat down next to His Holiness in front of the slow-burning logs. They both stared into the fire as they sipped on their tea and calmed their minds. The large windows gradually lit into an orange glow from the sunset outside before fading into darkness altogether. As the servants quietly circled the room lighting the chandeliers and clearing off the tables, Panchen moved from his chair onto the stone hearth in front of the fireplace, so that he was facing the Dalai Lama directly.

"We do not have to decide on our position right now," Panchen said softly. "Let's go to Shanghai and hear from all the attendants. We will prepare our position in accordance with our guiding doctrines of faith. If the situation dictates an alternative stance, we will respond accordingly."

The Dalai Lama was listening, but his mind appeared to be somewhere altogether different. "Panchen," he said. "Where were you when you attained total enlightenment?"

"Well, as you know, Your Holiness, full attainment comes in stages over a long period of time," he replied. "If one is disciplined and mindful of what lies beyond the ego-centric thought, he may experience moments of enlightenment throughout his life. I have certainly been one of those fortunate ones."

"Yes, no doubt you have, Panchen. As have I on more than one occasion. But where were you when you became a Buddha? When all the suffering's weight was lifted from your shoulders. When the light of truth completed you and answers no longer came from the teachings but came from your heart with the fearless conviction of a warrior!"

Panchen thought carefully about the question and his response. "My son," he said softly, "what you are asking is a conundrum of sorts. If I were to recall the moment when I became a Buddha, I would be exposing the duality of ultimate truth and self-awareness. To become a fully enlightened Buddha means there is no longer an 'I' and a 'Buddha'."

The two lamas sat quietly in deep thought.

The Dalai Lama finally spoke. "It feels like I am missing something. I have learned all the Buddhist tenets from you and the High Lamas. I have taken refuge in the Buddhist community and all of its principles and teachings. I have committed my life to the Noble Eight-fold Path. But I sense there is more," he said with open frustration. "When I see suffering in the world, I'm not sure I can fully connect with those feelings, and I become doubtful of my knowledge and ability to help."

"You're not missing anything, Gyatso. Your sincere compassion to serve is a noble attribute, and it pains you when you see such suffering in the world. Over time, you will proclaim the truths of Buddhism with an unwavering conviction, and the response from your loyal followers will supplant your doubts with joy and exuberance."

The two men sat quietly staring into the warm fire, contemplating their good fortune as simple monks in a simple world, and wondering how much longer that simplicity would last.

Gyatso rode his horse out to the edge of town where his father lived. When Gyatso was chosen as the next succession of the Dalai Lama over twenty years ago, he was an only child, living with his mother and father in a small village located in the valley next to Lhasa. The whole family was expected to move into the Potala palace, where they would receive exceptional treatment for the remainder of their lives. However, his parents declined the invitation to be relocated and chose to remain in their existing home, while making frequent trips into Lhasa to visit their son. This arrangement continued for several years until Gyatso's mother died after a prolonged illness. Gyatso's father then decided to move into a small farmhouse closer to Lhasa, but still refused the offer to reside in the Potala palace near his son. His father claimed that he wanted some land around him, to continue his farming tradition on some level. However, Gyatso knew that his father was simply too proud to accept such an offer from the government.

"Good morning father," said Gyatso as he dismounted his horse in front of a small vegetable garden being tilled and tended by his father. "I was heading out for a ride and thought you might like to come along."

"That would be wonderful, son. Let me clean up, and I will be ready to go."

The two men rode over into the next valley and then

followed a small creek up into the mountains. The trail eventually steepened considerably as it traversed around several large granite outcrops. Gyatso and his father dismounted and looked for a place to rest. Gyatso removed a cloth sack from his saddlebag, filled with snacks along with a flask of water. They found a flat place to sit that backed up to a large rock face protecting them from the relentless north winds and overlooked the beautiful sunlit valley below.

"I hear you are planning a trip to Shanghai," his father said.

"Yes, we are. It is an assembly of several South Asian countries. We hope to gain some consensus on the impacts facing our country's future."

"Sounds rather boring," his father said bluntly.

"Perhaps, but there are serious threats out there that could drastically change the political landscape as well as the comfortable lifestyles enjoyed by the Tibetan people."

"Blah, blah, blah," his father retorted mockingly.

"Yes, well, it may all sound rather trivial to you, but I happen to carry a sense of responsibility for the citizens of Tibet."

"Oh, I'm just teasing you, son. I know the burden you carry every day, and I know you have a genuine interest in the wellbeing of the people who look to you for guidance."

"Yes, I do. So, maybe you could show a little respect to your noble leader," Gyatso said sarcastically while trying to hide his grin.

The men both smiled at each other and then turned to look out at the natural richness in the valley below.

"Are you still having those nightmares?" his father asked.

"Yes," replied Gyatso in a somewhat frustrated tone. "Maybe not as often as before, but they seem to be getting stronger, or more frightful."

"In what way?"

"I don't know, I still dream about falling helplessly into darkness. But sometimes there is a bright light shining so hard, it seems to be pushing me off the edge." Gyatso paused to let his emotions settle. "Panchen believes it is youthful stress, and it will pass with time. Maybe he's right, but I feel like there is more to it. There are times when I struggle with my spiritual practice and I find myself filled with doubt." Gyatso paused when he felt the emotions swelling in his heart. "I sometimes wonder why it was me they chose to be their incarnated spiritual leader. What if they got it wrong?" Gyatso turned and looked out into the valley and discreetly wiped the tears from his eyes.

After a few minutes of silent thought, Gyatso's father spoke. "Your grandfather used to come up into these mountains when I was just a boy. I remember how he would be sitting at the table for breakfast some mornings and say, '*I need to go check on things.*' Then he would pack his horse and ride high up into these mountains all alone. He never told us where he was going, or when he would return. He would just disappear for several days. Then, when he did finally return, your grandmother would ask how everything went, and he would simply reply, *'Well, the universe is unfolding exactly as it should,'* and then he would laugh profusely."

"'The universe is unfolding exactly as it should,'" Gyatso contemplated the words as he repeated them. "What did he mean by that?"

Gyatso's father just shrugged his shoulders and smiled.

The trip to Shanghai was long and arduous. The Tibetan caravan consisted of five monks on horseback, including Panchen Lama; five yaks packed with supplies; two horse-drawn wagons for medical and weather-related relief; and seven servants who drove the yaks and wagons, helped set up camp and prepared meals along the trail. His Holiness was afforded a small but comfortable private carriage throughout the trip, but he preferred to ride horseback with the others most of the time. The road out of Lhasa was wide and well-traveled. However, this luxury quickly diminished as the caravan entered the isolated mountainous region between Tibet and coastal China. The beauty of the alpine tundra and snow-capped mountains was little consolation for the narrow, winding, and rugged path so painfully extending across the endless peaks and valleys. Eventually, the trail emerged from the mountains and deliberately poured out onto the verdant valley of the

Yangtze River. The river provided easy direction into Shanghai as well as a wonderful source of food, water, and accommodation from the small villages alongside the large, sinuous, and fertile vein of life.

The Tibetan delegates were graciously received by the government representatives of the Qing commission. Upon reaching the government offices in Shanghai, His Holiness was welcomed in person by the Qing Senior Ambassador along with an entourage of Chinese security, who expeditiously escorted the Tibetans through the congested city to a large government compound, complete with private hotel, fine restaurants, opulent gardens, and a lavish bathhouse for exclusive use by the Empire's visitors. The Tibetan visitors were welcomed into the hotel lobby, while the resort stewards attended to the traveler's livestock. The Qing Ambassador gave the Tibetans a personal tour of the grounds, explaining all the amenities and luxuries available to the guests. He then provided the Dalai Lama with an itinerary of meetings and scheduled events over the next few days before graciously excusing himself and leaving the visitors to settle into their private quarters. The lamas were free to enjoy the private compound and all its luxurious offerings. They were also free to leave the compound to explore the public activities along the riverside wharf. However, each visitor wishing to leave the compound was to be escorted by a security officer to ensure their safety and protection from peasants and peddlers in the city.

After a day or so of rest and recovery, the visitors were anxious to explore the city. Dressed in simple monk's robes early one evening, the Dalai Lama, Panchen, and a couple of monks were escorted down to the wharf, where the streets were filled with the eccentric sights, sounds, and smells of a large portside city. With music on almost every corner and endless rows of street vendors and food carts, the city was alive and vibrant with excitement. As the lamas walked down the wharf, they began to observe another side of the city. Dwelling in the darkness behind the vendors and below the pier were homeless vagrants, transients and rootless men and women, begging for food, while trying to keep their children warm and quiet. The smell of opium permeated the thick air along with hopeless poverty and vulnerability. As difficult as it was to observe, the lamas continued down the wharf, trying their best to stay close to the lit streets and mingling crowds. As the lamas reached the end of the pier, they observed a large steamship docked in the bay. Unlike anything they had ever seen, this ship stood several meters above the waterline, with towering masts and a web of guy-lines reaching high into the night sky. The ship's length seemed to extend forever into the bay before it disappeared completely into darkness. On the side of the massive ship was the name "Pacific Mail Steamship Company." The Tibetan visitors stood on the dock for several minutes in absolute astonishment at this new experience. When they turned to leave, they observed a sign propped along the side of the dock. The sign was posted in both Chinese and English and stated a departure date of "August 10" and a destination of "San Francisco, USA." Behind the sign was a small gathering of Chinese men waiting to obtain boarding documents the following morning. The lamas looked back at the massive steamship once more in amazement and then walked back up the wharf into the crowded streets and returned to their secured compound and private quarters for the evening.

The next few days were filled with meetings in the government compound. There were representatives from within the various regions of China as well as most of the surrounding countries, including Bhutan, Burma, Laos, and Vietnam. Led by the Qing commission, the topics focused almost exclusively on the increasing immigration of non-Asian citizens and their impact on the economic and social stability of South Asia. Anytime the conversation pointed to the Qing Dynasty as the cause for such problems or as an incapable regime to control such movements, the host commission swiftly redirected the agenda to a topic more central to everyone's interest. When it was time for each sovereign country to present its position on these foreign topics and a proposal on managing such impacts from abroad, the Dalai Lama stood and summarized the Tibetan position very succinctly.

"Tibet is a country geographically isolated from the goings-on of our neighbors. This isolation has, no doubt, brought its own register of difficulties and compromises for the Tibetan citizens," His Holiness stated with a shy grin. "However, we have yet to experience an influx of foreign visitors or the impacts they may bring to our communities. Regardless, we are not here to take sides or to take action against anyone. As a nation of Buddhist doctrines, it is our intention, individually and as a community, to seek alternatives to aggression and harmful actions. Rather, we will continue to show kindness, respect, and support to all our neighbors. And we will expect the same behavior in return."

The Qing commission patiently listened to the input from each of the countries. Then, with total disregard to what had been said by others, they returned to the podium and continued to press their agenda against outside influences, and how they intended to "protect" all their geographic neighbors from harm's way.

On the final day of the leadership summit, the Qing commission hosted an elaborate dinner party along with a festive ceremony celebrating the individual cultures throughout China. The next few days were spent preparing the Tibetan envoy for its return to Lhasa. On the morning of departure, the monks gathered outside along with a few other country delegates from the summit. There had been several friendly relationships established with other attendants over the course of the visit. There were genuine hugs and bows between new friends from neighboring countries, and everyone seemed to be in good spirits. The Dalai Lama had yet to come down from his private quarters at the hotel, so Panchen walked up the stairs to assist him with his baggage. After knocking a few times, Panchen opened the door to His Holiness' room. The bed was made, and the Dalai Lama's bags were all neatly packed and set on the floor next to the bed. Panchen called out once more to His Holiness, with no response. He walked to the back closet of the hotel room and peeked through the curtain. There was still no sign of the Dalai Lama. As he turned around, he saw a folded piece of paper lying on the nightstand, along with a string of prayer beads worn by His Holiness since he was a child. Holding the prayer beads in one hand and the note in the other hand, Panchen sat down on the bed, took a deep breath, and read the note.

> *My dearest Panchen, I will not be returning home with you today. After considerable thought and reflection, I have decided that I must venture out into the world so that I may experience the truth of human existence. I feel deeply that this is the only path for achieving full enlightenment. As the Buddha himself once said, "Knowledge is a process of self-discovery. You do not gain insight by accepting the opinions of others but by finding the truth within yourself."*
>
> *Tell the people of Tibet that I have set out to better understand the impacts of the 'New World,' so that I may return home and lead our families through the changing times ahead. I have no doubt the monastery will be in good hands and will prosper under your guidance. You are a true gift to all of Tibet and especially to me. You have been my father,*

*my teacher, my idol, and my friend, and I look
forward to my return soon.*
　Gyatso

　　Panchen folded the note into his lap and closed his eyes
in prayer. So many thoughts ran through his head, he
could hardly collect himself enough to leave. After several
minutes of deep thought, Panchen stood up, wiped the
tears from his eyes, gathered the bags of His Holiness, and
returned home to Lhasa.

CHAPTER FOUR

The decision to leave the Tibetan party in Shanghai was not one of impulse but rather a well thought out and prepared event by the Dalai Lama. Knowing that he would not be returning to Tibet for some time, the Dalai Lama brought his layman's clothing in his baggage, including field hat, sturdy boots, warm coat, and a money belt filled with gold and silver coins from the palace repository. The night before departing Shanghai, the Dalai Lama discretely ventured back down to the pier where the Pacific Mail Steamship Company ship was docked. It was there that he met a Chinaman who appeared to have just obtained documents for travel to America.

"Excuse me, sir, may I ask how you obtained those documents to travel on this ship?" the Dalai Lama asked in a broken Mandarin language.

"Quite simply," replied the Chinaman. "I signed up to work on the railroad in America, and they gave me a ticket aboard the ship."

"I see," replied the Dalai Lama. "I do not believe I am

in a position to obtain such documents, given my foreign status and lack of identification." The Dalai Lama then reached in his pocket and presented a gold coin to the Chinaman. "I wonder if I might buy your documents from you, kind sir?"

The Chinaman looked down at the gold coin in the Dalai Lama's hand. "Is that real?" asked the Chinaman staring at the coin with his eyes and mouth wide open.

"It sure is, sir," said the Dalai Lama, displaying the coin in his open hand. The Dalai Lama knew the coin was worth much more than the cost of the documents, and especially to the Chinaman laborer, who no doubt had never even seen a gold coin of this value. "Do we have a deal?"

"Oh my! Yes! Yes, we do have a deal!" exclaimed the Chinaman.

The documents were exchanged for the coin, and both men disappeared into the darkness of night.

The following morning, the Dalai Lama rose before sunrise, dressed in his layman's clothing, and snuck out of the compound and down to the shipping dock to board the vessel to America. As the Dalai Lama crossed over the boarding platform, he presented the documents to the American porter standing on the ship's stern. The porter glanced at the documents and then looked up at the Dalai Lama.

"Are you Li Xing?" asked the porter.

"Yes," the Dalai Lama whispered, hoping a whisper would lessen the severity of his lie.

The porter glanced once more at the documents and then directed Li downstairs. As Li proceeded down the narrow, winding stairs, the natural light was soon replaced with oil lamps located sparsely along the stairwell. At the lowest level of the ship was the steerage. The steerage compartment was located at the back of the ship and housed the steering mechanisms connecting the rudders to the tillers at the helm. The compartment itself was a large open section of the ship's hull. There was a low ceiling, requiring most men to lower their head while navigating, and a single row of oil lanterns running lengthwise down the middle. Heavy wooden planks were laid on the floor and the walls were exposed to the outer hull frame and completely absent of windows. There were iron-framed bunk beds placed around the perimeter of the room, each with a straw mattress, pillow, and a single blanket. Except for the bunk beds, a washbasin in one corner, and two privy buckets behind a curtain in another corner, there was no furniture anywhere in the compartment. Walking slowly beneath the lanterns, Li glanced side to side around the large room, trying to find an open bunk. The air in the room was thick, stale, and unbearable, forcing Li to cover his mouth and nose to hold back the gagging reflex. The bunks were filled with poverty-stricken Chinamen, all aiming to find their fortunes in America. As the conditions within China continued to deteriorate, America gave these men hope for a new life and a chance to succeed by working on the new frontier. Walking toward the back of the compartment, Li finally found a section with a few vacant beds and promptly claimed one for himself. After storing his bag under the bunk, he crawled onto the mattress and into the dark shadows. With his back to the wall and his knees curled tightly against his chest, His Holiness closed his eyes and tried to find solace in the dismal conditions in which he now found himself.

After a few minutes of privacy, another passenger approached. "Pardon me, pilgrim. You mind if I jump up here?" asked the man politely, pointing to the top bunk above Li.

Li opened his eyes and saw a young white man with a bag over his shoulder, pointing to the bunk above him. Though he did not understand English, Li pointed up to the bunk and nodded affirmatively to the man.

"Thanks," the man replied. He tossed his bag onto the top bunk and climbed up the iron frame at the foot of the bunk bed.

It wasn't long before a loud horn sounded from the top deck of the steamship, followed by a blast of steam and the loud rumblings of the paddlewheel turning water from under the bay. Li slipped back against the wall and into the shadows of the vessel. He could feel the ship gaining speed as the steam engine roared louder. Imagining the ship moving out to sea, Li was overcome with anxiety, knowing the safety of his surroundings was becoming more distant by the moment. His thoughts vacillated between the land

and the sea; between the known and the unknown; between the past and the future. He thought of Panchen riding back to Lhasa without him and how the High Lamas would react to the news he carried. He thought of Lobsang back home and the comfort he provided with his friendship all these years. He thought of his father and so hoped that he would support his son's decision and be proud of his independence. He thought of the simple privileges he enjoyed at the palace, and how he would miss them. Before drifting completely into self-pity, Li caught himself and opened his eyes to regain touch with reality.

After a couple of hours at sea, the ship's stewards brought in several large kettles of rice, along with containers of hot tea and utensils. The stewards placed everything on the floor at the foot of the stairwell, then immediately returned to the upper decks. After a few moments of stillness, the Chinamen rose simultaneously and gathered around the rice bowls. What looked at first like chaos, quickly turned into a coordinated effort of polite respect and discipline. Within minutes, every Chinaman had been served a bowl of rice, with a spoon and a cup of hot tea, and returned to their bunks to eat. There were a few stragglers who came up later to fill their bowls, including Li and the American residing on the top bunk above him. When the two men returned to their bunks, the American sat on the floor next to Li's bed and introduced himself.

"How do you do, sir? My name is Elliot," said the

American, speaking in Mandarin as he stuck out his hand toward Li.

Elliot was a tall man, with blonde hair combed neatly back over his head. He had a scruffy beard, blue eyes, and a friendly smile. He wore a well-pressed collared shirt, dark slacks with narrow black suspenders stretching over his broad shoulders.

"Elliot," repeated Li. "My name is Li," he said and reached over to shake the extended hand.

"Pleased to meet you, Li," said Elliot. "Do you speak English?"

"No," replied Li.

"Well, I speak enough Mandarin for us to get along, I expect," said Elliot

"Thank you," said Li, nervously hoping he knew as much Mandarin as the American did.

The two bunkmates sat quietly eating their first meal together. Elliot had a generous smile and seemed to be very content, given the conditions of their surroundings.

"Are you going to America to get rich in the gold rush?" asked Elliot in a farcical sort of way.

"No, I go to America to work on the railroad."

"Oh yeah, the Iron Horse."

The men returned to their bowls, quietly eating, and looking around the room at all the other passengers on board. Several of the Chinamen had taken their empty bowls over to the washbasin and cleaned them thoroughly before returning to their bunks.

Elliot finished his rice and stood up. "Best to keep your own utensils. Might not see any more for a while," said Elliot to Li. "We can clean them over here," he said pointing to the washbasin.

The two men stood and walked over to the washbasin to clean their utensils. Li wondered how it was that Elliot knew all the ins and outs of the ship. When they returned to their bunks, Elliot climbed up onto his bed. Li placed his utensils into his bag and stood up next to Elliot's bunk.

"What do you do in China?" he asked.

"Well Mr. Li," replied Elliot. "I am a Christian missionary." Elliot paused and looked at Li for a response. "Do you know what a Christian is?"

"Yes, I know a little about your religion. Mostly from the teachings I received in my school years."

"Well, perhaps we can give you a little refresher course over the next few weeks," Elliot said with a smile. "It just so happens I have an extra Bible in my bag."

Elliot stretched out on his bed and closed his eyes to nap. Li watched Elliot for another moment, and then retreated to his own bunk and resumed his position sitting in the darkness against the wall.

Over the next couple of days, the Chinamen travelers sorted themselves into distinct groups. Most of them preferred to assemble at one end of the compartment where opium was widely available and shared throughout the day. These men rarely went up on deck, preferring to remain below, sleeping in their beds, or gathering on the floor smoking opium and conversing among themselves. Those who had yet to succumb to opium gathered in another area, drinking tea, socializing, and playing cards or dominoes. The rest of the compartment travelers spent as much time as possible on the upper deck, where fresh air and sunlight were precious resources. There were tables and benches set out for socializing, reading, and playing games. It took Li a day or two to adjust to his new surroundings. His routine had been completely disrupted and, feeling sorry for himself, he preferred to be alone most of the time. He would spend as much time as possible on the open deck, either reading his scriptures, meditating, or simply resting over a cup of hot tea. Then one morning, during one of his readings, he came across a proverb he learned in school:

> *If you are sorrowful, you are living in the past.*
> *If you are anxious, you are living in the future.*
> *If you are at peace, you are living in the present.*

The Dalai Lama had read this proverb dozens of times in the past. But it wasn't until today that its meaning resonated so brilliantly. As he closed his eyes and thought deeper about this passage, he realized that he had been completely absorbed in self-pity and anxiety ever since the ship left the dock. His longing for the safety of his past and the fear of his unknown future completely dominated his thoughts and emotions. As soon as he came to this realization, he could feel a weight lifted from his shoulders and a tension released throughout his body. When he opened his eyes, he found everything around him was somehow brighter and fresher than before. The sea was a vibrant mix of beautiful green tones as it floated into the distant horizon and met up with a most spectacular blue sky filled to infinity. The Chinamen sitting around the deck appeared happier and more engaged in their games. The ship's stewards were all smiling and conversing as they did their chores. Li was thrilled with his discovery and could not help but smile as he enjoyed the new view through the window of his mind.

One day, while Li was enjoying his morning tea on the upper deck, Elliot emerged from the stairs and approached Li, holding a Bible in his hand. He laid the Bible down in front of Li.

"I hope you will accept this as a gesture of our new friendship, without any expectations or obligations from you," Elliot said politely.

"Thank you, Elliot," replied Li. "I am very grateful for the gift, and for your friendship." As Li lifted the Bible and fingered through a few pages, an idea entered his mind. "Elliot, do you suppose you could teach me to speak English, using the Bible as a reference?"

Elliot thought for a moment. Then, with a huge grin on his face, he replied, "I most certainly can! Not only am I a Bible-loving Christian, but I am also an English graduate from Dartmouth College!"

Li couldn't help but smile back at the huge grin pasted on Elliot's face.

"Very well then. Perhaps we can start tonight."

The two men stood up and shook hands, and then turned to gaze out onto the beautiful ocean expanding into the distant horizon.

The next several days passed rather quickly as Li and Elliot settled into a daily routine of reading and speaking English while reading about Jesus Christ and all his disciples. One day, while the two men practiced speaking English, Elliot asked a question to Li. "Why do you have a shaved head, Li? It seems so different than the long queues of the other Chinamen?"

Li was startled a bit by the question and wasn't quite sure how to answer. He thought quickly about how to answer as truthfully as he could.

"I was sent to a religious school as a youth, where we were required to maintain short hair. I keep it that way now because it is simple and requires little effort," replied Li.

"So, you were raised as a Buddhist?" Elliot asked knowingly.

"Yes, I was raised as a Buddhist."

"Fascinating," said Elliot. "I always found Buddhism difficult to argue against in my religious debates in school. Its attention to virtue, kindness, and moderation as a source of fulfillment is so simple, it cannot be denied," Elliot stated with a bewildered tone.

"I agree," said Li with a thoughtful smile.

The trip across the Pacific was long and monotonous. Every day seemed like a replay of the day before. The English lessons were a welcome distraction from the daily boredom of ship life. Li and Elliot spent hours in readings and discussions and became rather close friends during the trip. The Bible used by Li over the weeks had become worn and tattered, and filled with notes from Elliot's lessons. Li had become fairly competent with the English language, though he continued to struggle with word contractions and slang words. On the last day before docking into San Francisco harbor, Elliot gave Li his final lesson.

"I guess I should return this to you now," Li said, extending the worn Bible to Elliot.

"Don't be ridiculous, Li, that is your Bible forever now. Besides, it's practically unreadable, with all those funny words you wrote in it!"

"Thank you, Elliot. I will keep this as a token of our friendship."

"Well, I hope you will read it often and refer to it as a guide through difficult times," Elliot said.

"I must say," Li stated. "I do find Jesus to be a most interesting person. And I see his message of love, compassion, and forgiveness quite similar to many of my religious leaders."

"I'll take that as a hopeful sign!" Elliot said as he extended both arms out to embrace his friend.

CHAPTER FIVE

As the ship approached land in America, the energy and excitement of the passengers and crew were lifted to new heights. Even the opium clan came out from the steerage compartment to enjoy the fresh air and view of the American port from the upper deck. Looking out across the bay, Li could see the docks full of people, rushing back and forth, pushing carts, pulling wagons, walking horses, and conducting business. Suddenly, the reality of what he was about to do sank in, and a wave of nervous anxiety flushed through his body. He had been thinking about this moment for months, but never really considered what it would feel like to step foot onto American soil.

With a soft thud, the steamship collided with buoys tied to the dock. Several shore men began catching ropes tossed from the ship's crew and tying them to the anchor posts along the dock. With the ship secured, the stewards lowered the ramp onto the dock and opened the gate to allow the travelers to disembark. Elliot was waiting for Li at the bottom of the ramp.

"I think you will need to stop by the Immigration Office for further directions," said Elliot, sensing the confusion in Li's eyes. "You will see the building when you get over to Main Street," he said, pointing toward the intersection.

"Thank you, Elliot," said Li. "This is all very unfamiliar at the moment."

"Don't worry about a thing. You will be just fine."

The two men shook hands one final time. Then Elliot turned and walked into the bustling city.

Li began walking toward Main Street, alongside some other Chinamen from the ship when he heard some yelling from up the street.

"Go back home, you bloody coolies!" yelled a man from the corner as he threw a rock toward the docks.

"We don't need your wretched kind around here!" said another man, as he launched an empty liquor bottle into the crowd.

The Chinamen, sensing danger, scattered in all directions, trying to disappear into the crowded city. Li found himself running behind another Chinaman toward an alley off the main docks. As they entered the alley and stopped to look back, a rock suddenly smashed into Li's head, knocking him to the ground.

"Get up!" yelled the Chinaman. "We have to get into Chinatown."

Li was dazed from the blow to his head. He reached up and felt the blood streaming down his neck. He was not sure he could run any further. He glanced up at the Chinaman.

"How far is it?" Li asked.

"This way, not far!" exclaimed the Chinaman, as he pulled Li up from the ground.

The two men hurried through the alley and out onto the open street toward Chinatown. They ran until they could no longer hear the hoodlums yelling. When they stopped to look back, they found no attackers, and the danger appeared to have diminished. Li bent over with his hands on his knees and tried to catch his breath. He was still dizzy and disoriented from the injury and could see the blood dripping off his neck onto the ground. When he finally regained his breath, he stood up to find the Chinaman had disappeared.

Li looked around for the Chinaman and discovered that, while the man was nowhere to be found, other Chinamen filled the streets all around him. Horse-drawn wagons rattled down the dusty streets, and the sidewalks were filled with Chinese pedestrians busily coming and going. There were food carts in the streets selling Chinese food, and even some well-dressed Chinamen conducting business along the wood-planked sidewalks. The stores all had Chinese names, with elaborate window displays filled with Chinese goods. Chinese shoppers strolled casually up and down both sides of the street looking to spend their hard-earned money.

Li felt another wave of dizziness in his head and

quickly moved off the busy street and sat down under a wooden canopy behind one of the vendor shops. His top robe was soaked in blood, so he removed it and tore off a cloth strip to tie against the head wound and stop the bleeding. He then reached into his pack, removed his warm coat, and put it on over his bare skin. He sat on the sidewalk for several minutes, trying to regain his orientation. Li figured it was too late to try and find the Immigration Office, and he was in no condition to ask for help. As he walked slowly down the walkway, trying to find a place of refuge, he noticed some men walking into a small open area underneath a balcony between two old buildings. Li followed them into the opening and quickly moved to the back corner. He sat with his back against one wall, lifted his pack above his shoulder and rested his head against the pack on the other wall. Even though it was dark, he closed his eyes so that he could not see the others in the room. He heard yelling back and forth from several men playing Fan-Tan in one corner, and he could smell the sweet scent of opium, as it filled the air from another corner. Li was tired, hungry, and scared, and his head was throbbing from the wound. He lay down onto the dirt floor and tried to relax, but his body would not stop shivering. He curled up tighter, trying to cease the violent shaking, but it only got worse. The convulsions continued uncontrollably until his body finally shut down from shock and he passed out completely.

The sun was just coming up when a man walked under the balcony and yelled at all the squatters.

"Get up, you lazy bums! This is not a hotel. Get up and get out. Now!" said the man as he walked around in a circle, kicking the bodies on the ground.

The loud noise woke Li from a deep sleep. He lifted his head and tried to see who was yelling. His head was throbbing with pain and he stumbled aimlessly as he stood up, gathered his belongings, and staggered out of the darkness into the morning light. Li felt the crusted bandage on his head. He knew he must have dried blood all over his face. He quickly glanced up and down the street, looking for a place to clean himself. He noticed a horse trough around the corner and moved swiftly toward the water as he removed the bandage from his head. Cupping his hands, he splashed his head, face, and neck enough to scrub the blood off. He dried his face with the torn robe and then tore off another cloth strip to apply a dry bandage to the head wound. He put on his field hat to cover the bandage and splashed a couple of handfuls of fresh water into his mouth, to get both a cleansing and a drink before returning to the street.

Li looked for the Immigration Office, but the throbbing in his head, his hunger, and his general fear and anxiety made it difficult for him to think straight or to translate the signs along the streets. He eventually approached a Chinese vendor who was busy opening his store.

"Excuse me, sir, can you tell me where the

Immigration Office is?" Asked Li.

The Chinaman looked up from his busywork, glanced at Li with a scowl on his face, and then pointed to a large government building across the street.

"Thank you, kind sir," Li said and walked across the street and into the building. Once inside, he found the Immigration Office and proceeded to the front desk.

"Credit-ticket," said the American man without even looking up.

"Pardon me?" replied Li.

"Credit-ticket," said the man again, this time pointing to a sample ticket pinned to the countertop.

Li quickly recognized the sample and reached into his pack for his document.

"Are you Li Xing?" asked the man reading over the details in the document.

"Yes, sir, I am," replied Li nervously.

"You understand that the railroad company paid for your ticket over here, and you will not be paid for any day's work until the price for the ticket has been repaid," the man recited to Li in a routine voice.

Li suddenly realized that he had been duped into paying for a free ticket on the steamship back in Shanghai. Before Li could respond, the man gave him a sheet containing an address with directions to the San Francisco Transit Station.

"This is where you will board the train to Sacramento. Here is your ticket," the man said as he slid the ticket across the counter. "And here is a voucher for $10 at the General Store down the street," the man said as he pointed out the door. "The store has a list of items you will need to buy. The train to Sacramento leaves every morning at 9 a.m. Any questions?" the man asked as he turned and walked into the backroom.

Li tried his best to process the information, but it all came out so fast. With the man now gone into the backroom, Li was left with no choice but to leave the office. He gathered all the documents and exited out onto the sidewalk to try and understand what had just happened.

After a few minutes of looking over the documents, he had a better understanding of the instructions he was given. He proceeded across the street to the General Store, where he presented his $10 voucher and told the storekeeper he was going to work on the railroad. The storekeeper walked around the store grabbing items off the shelves and placing them on the countertop, before crossing the item off from the list in his hand.

"This is what you get for $10," the man stated. "Anything else is extra."

Li looked over the items. There was a bedroll, wool blanket, boots, large brim hat, work gloves, canteen, one pair of slacks with suspenders, one work shirt, and a heavy coat. Deciding that he already owned better boots and a warm coat, and needing money for food, Li removed the boots and coat from the assembly and asked for the change instead. The storekeeper put the remaining items into a bag and handed Li $2 in change. With the change in his hand, Li walked over to the food shelves and filled one sack full of hardtack biscuits and another with dried fruit.

"Is this two dollars?" asked Li.

"I reckon so," replied the storekeeper, feeling generous toward the friendly foreigner. The storekeeper added the food items to Li's bag and took the rest of his money.

"Good luck, pilgrim," said the storekeeper.

"Thank you, kind sir," said Li as he bowed and walked out the door.

With his documents in hand and a bag full of supplies, Li felt better about his situation. However, his head still ached and throbbed continuously, and he needed a clean bath and rest before he ventured out to the railroad site. He also realized that he was going to be working without pay for some time until his debts to the railroad were paid off. Li walked back out onto the busy streets of Chinatown. The streets were once again bustling with Chinese shoppers, peddlers, and vendors. He began walking along the sidewalk, looking for a bank where he could convert one of his coins into cash currency, and for a hotel where he could clean up and rest.

After Li had checked into the hotel, cleaned his wounds thoroughly and eaten some biscuits and dried fruit for dinner, he lay down on the soft bed to rest. Li closed his eyes and tried to calm the turmoil winding through his mind. The past couple of days had been extremely challenging. Li suddenly felt the emotional impact of being so far from his homeland. His chest tightened when he realized that he had no idea where he was nor where he was going. All he knew for sure was that he was nowhere close to home, and he would be boarding a train tomorrow destined for somewhere even farther away. Doubt suddenly began to race through his head. The culture he found himself immersed in appeared to have no resemblance to his people or his upbringing. Perhaps there are no redeeming values to be learned from the Americans, he thought. And it appeared there was little interest by the Americans in what he had to offer. When Li was planning this trip to America, he imagined it would be a new and challenging experience, but never did he imagine it would be filled with such hate and violence that his life would be at risk. Restless with doubts and anxiety, Li closed his eyes and took a few deep breaths to settle his emotions. After several minutes of quiet contemplation, Li regained his sense of control and put himself to sleep, knowing tomorrow would be a big day.

Li woke up the following morning clean and refreshed. His head wound felt much better, and his new clothes made him feel like a new man. He packed his supplies into his bedroll and ventured downstairs. He sat on the sidewalk steps while he ate some biscuits and read the directions he had been given to the transit station. The station was located a few blocks outside of Chinatown, and Li was leery of the encounter he had down at the docks when he first arrived. He tucked his fruit and biscuits into his pack, secured everything tightly to his body and proceeded cautiously out of Chinatown to the transit station.

CHAPTER SIX

The train ride to Sacramento was most enjoyable. Li was fascinated with the size and power of the steam engine and the number of railcars the engine was able to pull. He felt like a kid sitting upright in his seat with his head perched out the window taking in all the sights, sounds and smells. And getting out of the city and into the open country brought a fresh perspective to Li and renewed his excitement for what was ahead. The train pulled into Sacramento and the passengers proceeded to exit. A large man stood on the platform next to the train with a sign that read, "Central Pacific Railroad Workers." When Li approached the man, he was directed to a group of men gathered at the end of the platform next to a large horse-drawn wagon. After all the passengers had disembarked from the train, the large man strolled over to the men gathered at the wagon.

"Howdy, fellows," the man said politely. "This here wagon is going to the worksite for the Central Pacific Railroad. If you have a ticket to work for the railroad, hop on up there. If you don't, then you're in the wrong line."

Li and six other men climbed onto the open wagon and settled onto a bench on either side, storing their bags under the bench.

"Well, okay then," said the driver, as he climbed up onto the front bench and grabbed the reins leading to two large draft horses. "Let's hit the road."

The passengers on the wagon were all men. Four of the men were Chinese, all dressed in cotton trousers and loose-fitting shirts along with straw conical hats typical of Chinese farmers. It appeared the Chinamen all opted for cash instead of spending their $10 vouchers on supplies: perhaps another financial oversight by the naïve traveler from Tibet. The other two were white men dressed in work jeans, shirts and wool vests. They both wore short-brimmed derby hats typical of the Irish emigrant. There were some brief introductions and small talk, but mostly the Chinamen kept to themselves, as did the Irishmen.

It was dark when the wagon arrived at the worksite. There were a couple of small campfires illuminating the faces of a few workers, but the rest of the camp appeared to have already gone down for the evening. The driver pulled up to the main camp and the passengers all gathered their bags and exited out the back of the wagon, where they were greeted by one of the workers.

"Good evening, gentlemen. My name is Jesse," the man said with a slow drawn out accent. "I'm one of the foremen working on this crew. The kitchen is over there, and I believe Cookie left y'all some rice and beans. You can lay down your bed anywhere you like. Probably up there would be best," he said pointing to a flat opening near the trees. "Breakfast bell rings at 6 a.m. Work crews will start leaving at 7 a.m. We'll get you all on a team in the morning. So, get some rest," Jesse said as he turned and walked over to one of the campfires.

The newcomers all moved quickly toward the kitchen wagon, hoping for a hot meal. Li was served a bowl of rice and proceeded over to the flat opening near the trees. He sat down on his bag next to another Chinaman from the trip today.

"Your name is Shen. Is that correct?" Li asked politely.

"Yes," replied Shen. "You are Li?" asked the Chinaman in broken English.

"Yes," Replied Li. "Do you speak English?"

"Very little," replied Shen.

They both smiled and began eating. Shen was a young, very perceptive man, with a lean frame, bright smile, and a long, braided queue down his back. He appeared to be traveling alone and was not at all nervous or intimidated by his surroundings. Li and Shen continued to make small talk during dinner but were both anxious to get a good night's sleep after a long day of travel.

The next morning, the new arrivals were called over to the foreman's meeting for their team assignments. Jesse had the list of names in his hand but preferred to use his judgment for assigning teams.

"You, you, and you," Jesse said pointing to three of the Chinamen. "Go over there with John. The rest of you go see Paddy," he said pointing to a short man with a straight back, bulging belly and a full mustache with a hint a gray.

Li, Shen, and the two Irishmen all moved over next to Paddy. The other three Chinamen left with Foreman John. Jesse then walked over to get the names crossed off his list and make the introductions to their new bosses.

Paddy made a point to shake each new worker's hand while giving him a good look in the eye. He said he could tell a lot by a handshake and a smile on a fellow. The two Irishmen, Mick and Ross, felt empowered by their relational heritage to their new boss and showed a relaxed and friendly posture as they spoke to Paddy. Li and Shen each offered a firm handshake and a smile, but otherwise kept a low profile with their new team. With the formalities complete, the workers filled their canteens, grabbed their hat and gloves, and went to work.

Railroad work was hard work, and the days were long. Paddy's team worked mostly on laying down new track. This was not as dirty of a job as blasting and excavation but required a strong back to lift long sections of steel track and swing a sledgehammer all day. The crews pretty much worked sunup to sundown, seven days per week. It took Li several days to adjust to the workload and get used to sore muscles and exhaustion at the end of every day.

In time, Li started to feel a level of calm and comfort

in his new surroundings. His center of focus was no longer on the struggles for survival, allowing him to be more receptive to the holistic experience. He began to look more at the natural beauty of the surrounding mountains and valleys. The mountains, though significantly smaller, reminded him of his home back in Lhasa, which filled him with fond memories and gratitude. The valleys, however, were lush, green and filled with an endless assortment of spectacular wildflowers, unlike anything he ever saw in the high elevations of Tibet. He found time in the evenings for quiet reflection and meditation; something that had been missing for several weeks now. He no longer felt the anxiety of what was ahead or the pangs for what he left behind. Instead, he became fully engaged with the richness of his new life and the beauty it presented each day.

Eventually, everyone fell into a routine of long days on the rails, followed by dinner, small talk, and maybe a card game before seeking out a good night's sleep in preparation for the next day. While the nights were mostly quiet, there was ongoing tension between the Irishmen and the Chinamen. The Irish displayed a position of entitlement that set them apart from the Chinamen. Their status on the team was perceived as one of superiority over the Chinamen, often leading to verbal abuse, situational conflict and sometimes violence. The Chinamen were much harder workers than the Irishmen, making the situation even more contentious. For the most part, Paddy was able to contain the outbursts of the Irish workers and would move the Chinamen to a separate section of rails when necessary to keep a situation from escalating.

When the railroad construction was close to a town, the crews would stop work on Saturday morning and hitch up a couple of wagons to ride into town for the weekend. The men looked forward to a clean shower, soft bed, and a little fun and games in the town saloon. Li and Shen usually elected to go into town, mainly for the hot shower and soft beds. However, many of the towns they passed through were so small and remote that Chinamen were still a relatively new experience to the locals. The foremen all made a point to lecture the Chinamen about the possibility of trouble in town and were adamant about keeping away from intoxicated white men at all costs.

As the teams finished up their morning routine, they gathered over by the foreman's wagon to collect their wages for the week and listen to the upcoming plans for the weekend.

"Right now, we are about ten miles outside of Reno," Jesse stated to the crews during their morning briefing. "Once we reach the Reno Station, we will be connecting with another rail line and then move on east from there."

This excited the men, as Reno was one of the larger towns, which meant there would be ladies. And, it meant that the layover would be more than a few days, while the lines were connecting to the station.

"All right fellows, listen up," Jesse hollered, trying to

regain everyone's attention. "We have enough ties and track to get us into Reno, except for the spikes. Apparently, they left those crates off the last delivery, and they are due to arrive later today. So, Paddy will leave a team of 'spikers' behind to wait for the delivery and then spike the rails on into town," Jesse finished and then released everyone into their work teams.

Paddy was filling his canteen when Mick and Ross both approached him.

"Paddy, we don't want to be stayin' behind waitin' on them bloody spikes to arrive!" exclaimed Mick. "That means we don't get into town for two or three more days. While everyone else is a hoopin' and a hollerin' up a storm with them saloon girls!"

"Well, hell boys! Just what would you suggest I do?" said Paddy. "Someone needs to stay behind and wait for them spikes. And you two are part of the spiker team. So, you two are gonna have to wait!"

"What about leaving the coolies behind? They're part of the spiker team too," said Mick in protest.

"Oh, they're staying behind too," informed Paddy. "It's gonna take two teams to get caught up with the rest of the crew."

"Dammit-to-hell Paddy! This ain't fair!" Mick cried out.

"Well, if it makes you feel any better, you'll be gettin' paid for sittin' on your bloody arse waiting for them spikes to arrive," Paddy said.

"Oh, hell no, that don't make me feel no better!" cried Mick. "I'd still rather be in town."

"Well, I'm sorry fellas," Paddy said. "But it is what it is, and that's the way it's gonna be."

The four spikers stood on the tracks and watched as the rest of the crew moved down the hill, dropping ties and laying rails toward town. Li and Shen moved on over to the camp and settled down under the shade, while the two Irishmen continued to watch in bitter envy until the crew was completely out of sight.

"Bloody hell! This ain't no fair!" Mick cried out, as he heaved a rock in violent frustration toward the work crews. The two Irishmen then turned and walked up to the camp and sat down in an angry protest.

The Irishmen chose to sleep away the day while waiting for the spikes to arrive. Li and Shen took a walk up to a small stream leading through a grassy valley and into the forest. The men sat quietly alongside the stream bank watching the water flow by.

"Do you have a family back at home?" asked Shen.

"No," replied Li. "Except for my father, who lives in my town. Do you have a family back home, Shen?"

"Yes, I have a wife and baby son," Shen answered. "As soon as my child was born, I knew I needed to earn more money to support him," he said. "There are no jobs in my town. My wife works at her father's laundry, and we live in the back of the shop," Shen said with a tone of disgrace. "I came here to earn enough money to start a new life for my family."

"I appreciate your devotion to family, Shen," said Li.

"There are no stronger ties than with a child."

Li paused for a moment to think about his response. "It has always been my observation that true love is more powerful than anything else in this world. And no amount of money can buy true love," he said slowly to Shen.

"I know," said Shen with tears in his eyes. "But I want him to be proud of his father."

"Yes, and I have no doubts that he is very proud of his father," said Li, sensing despair in Shen's reply.

Shen stood up and started walking slowly down the hill toward camp. Li remained seated by the stream, giving Shen some needed privacy.

Back at camp, the Irishmen had started a fire and heated some chili left by Cookie. They had already eaten dinner and were busy sipping on a flask of whiskey when Li arrived. The load of spikes had arrived on a horse-drawn railcar sometime before sunset.

"Okay, mates, now that we are all here," Mick announced as he stood up. "As you can see, the spikes have arrived. Which means that we can now start spiking the rails towards town. Ross and I have been doin' some thinkin'. If we can get a good start tonight, we should be able to finish up before dark tomorrow. That way, we can be in town with the rest of the fellas tomorrow night," Mick said in a friendly and positive tone.

Shen already had a bowl of chili and was seated near

the fire. Li walked over to the fire, spooned him out some chili, tore off a piece of bread and sat down next to Shen.

"So, fellas, what do you say?" asked Ross, looking over at the Chinamen.

Li and Shen proceeded to eat their dinner while thinking about the Irishmen's proposal. Li wiped his mouth with his sleeve before replying.

"If we try to spike rails in the dark, it will be very slow going. And I cannot see us getting very far tonight," Li said. "Also, I think we could easily cause an injury to one of us, potentially a very serious injury."

"Oh, that's a load of bullshit, Li!" exclaimed Mick. "We been spiking so long; we could do this in our bloody sleep!"

Li chose to remain quiet, so as not to provoke Mick further.

Mick looked at Shen. "What about you Shen? Are you up for getting a head start tonight?"

"I have to agree with Li," Shen replied. "There are too many risks to justify working while in the dark."

"Oh shit!" cried Mick. "What a bunch of Goddamn sissies!" Mick grabbed the flask from Ross and took a swig.

Li stood up and walked over to rinse his bowl.

"You know, we don't have to wait for you two sissies. We can start anytime we want," Mick said as he watched Li walk by him.

"Maybe that would be good," Shen said with a smile. "Then we could catch up to you in the morning."

Shen looked over at Li, and they both smiled at each

other.

"Ha! Ha! You frickin' coolie," Mick snapped back defensively. "Maybe you'd like to place a little wager on that!"

A moment of tension came over the camp, and the men all sat down, quietly staring at the fire. Finally, Ross broke the silence.

"Just what would you be proposin', Mick?" Ross said with genuine interest.

"We take the left track and the Chinamen take the right track," Mick stated. "We split up the spikes onto two rail carts. Whoever is in front uses the front cart. The first team to reach town wins."

The camp fell quiet again, while the idea settled into the men's thoughts. Shen looked over at Li for some sort of a signal. Li could tell that Shen was interested in the proposal. After a few more moments, Li broke the silence and spoke directly to Shen.

"I am not a gambling man, Shen. And it is not in my nature to make foolish wagers," he said as delicately as he could.

Shen stood up and nervously walked over next to Li.

"You know we can beat them, Li," Shen whispered. "I do not think it is such a foolish wager."

"If it is important to you, I will do my best to help you," Li whispered back to Shen. "But you must make this decision for yourself."

Mick could tell that Shen was interested and offered

some more details.

"So, we all just got paid this morning, right?" Mick stated. "What do you say we all pitch in one week's wages, and winners take all?"

Shen thought some more about the wager. "And we all start at sunrise?" Shen clarified the proposal.

"Fine with me, mate," Mick conceded.

There was another pause, as everyone looked around the fire at each other, just waiting. Suddenly, Mick lit up a grin, as Shen reached out to shake his hand.

"Whoa!!" Ross let out with a burst. "I think we gotta' bloody race comin' tomorrow!" he said, looking over at Mick with a huge grin of his own.

Li stood up and shook hands with Mick and Ross. He then walked back over to Shen, shook his hand and said, "We best get some rest, my friend."

Mick, hearing the reply from Li interjected. "Well, first we gotta' be sealin' the deal!" he said, as he held out the flask to Li.

"The deal has been made, Mick," Li stated firmly, without showing intimidation.

"Fine! Go on to bed, you bloody tot!" Mick said as he sat down and handed the flask over to Ross.

Li and Shen walked over to their bedrolls and tried to settle down enough to get to sleep. Li felt horrible about the wager. He thought perhaps he should have been more influential in talking Shen out of the deal. He could have simply said that it was against his religion, and everything would have ended right then. Li could not see any good coming to them tomorrow. If they win, Mick and Ross will be angry and will most likely act out on their anger, suffering additional consequences. If they lose, it will be devastating to Shen, losing a whole week of wages. Li finally concluded that he also would suffer from bad karma either way. He closed his eyes and prepared himself as best he could for what was ahead.

"Guess we'll see you two losers in town!" Mick said as the four men walked down to the tracks.

"You know it's over ten miles into town." Li reminded Mick.

"Yeah. So, what are you saying?" Mick snapped back.

"I doubt we have ever done ten miles in a day, that's all," said Li.

"Well then, we'll be in town, whenever you two sissies get there!" Mick replied.

The four men had each put one week's wages into a canvas bag and secured it to the first rail cart along with half of the spikes from the delivery. Mick and Ross pushed the front cart onto the rails and prepared the first spike on the left track. The Irishmen took off quickly ahead of the Chinamen, establishing a fast pace from the start. Li pushed the second cart of spikes onto the rails and waited for the Irishmen to get out of the hearing range.

"How do you feel, Shen?" Li asked casually.

"Fine, Li," said Shen as he looked anxiously at the

Irishmen down the track. "But they're getting ahead, while we are talking!"

"Relax, Shen. We have a long day ahead of us," Li stated calmly. He reached into his bedroll on the rail cart and pulled out a sack of dried biscuits. He took one biscuit and presented the sack to Shen. "Get some food in you, Shen. We must keep something in our stomachs all day to avoid exhausting our energy." Shen took a biscuit out of the sack and took a bite while continuing to look nervously down the tracks.

"It is also very important that we drink water throughout the day," Li continued. "I will take the sledge to start. You can set the spikes. If you can set up the spikes with one good hammer hit, it will allow me to use a consistent stroke to drive them down with the sledge."

"Okay," said Shen as he grabbed a small hammer from the rail cart.

Shen set up his first spike on the right-side rails and then moved down to set another. Li grabbed the sledgehammer from the back of the cart and watched Shen for several minutes. He then put on his gloves and drove his first spike into the rails with four swings of the sledgehammer. He repeated the action on the next few spikes until he was able to drive the spike down with only three swings of the sledge. Once he established a three-strike rhythm, he settled into a steady pace, allowing Shen to also establish a steady pace in front of him. Even though Li and Shen were moving well, they were not catching up with Mick and Ross. The Irish team continued to move farther ahead and were soon completely out of sight from the Chinamen.

After a couple of hours into the workday, Shen paused for a drink and waited for Li to catch up.

"I haven't seen those men for some time. What do you think?" Shen said as he scooped a cup of water from the rail cart and handed it to Li. Li took a drink from the cup and then looked down the tracks toward the Irishmen.

"I think they are pushing themselves pretty hard," Li replied. "If they can keep that pace all day, they will have earned their winnings."

"Are you ready to switch off yet?" Shen asked Li.

"No, not yet. I feel good," Li replied, trying to give Shen some confidence. The two Chinamen wiped the sweat from their faces, poured some cold water down their backs and got back to work. The men quickly ramped back up to a steady pace. As the day lingered on, Shen offered several times to switch places with Li, but it became apparent that Li was not going to give up the sledge. He had decided last night that the best outcome from this race would be to win it for Shen's sake and then try to manage the Irishmen's reactions as best he could.

It was early afternoon when Shen rounded a corner and once again saw the two Irishmen some distance away at the end of the valley.

"I see them!" hollered Shen back to Li. Li paused and looked up to see Shen pointing down the tracks with broad a smile on his face.

"Just as we planned," hollered Li, feeling somewhat relieved by the news. The Chinamen continued to slowly gain on the Irishmen until the Irishmen finally stopped working altogether. Shen continued to set spikes until he reached the other cart in front of him, and then waited for Li. The Chinamen laid down their tools, grabbed some water and walked over to the grassy hillside where Mick and Ross had collapsed.

"So, this is Reno!" exclaimed Li jokingly, as he looked around the tree-lined hillside.

"Yeah, very funny!" Mick snapped back. "We just thought we'd take a little rest and let you two coolies catch up a bit."

"Oh, that is very nice of you!" Li replied. "You do not mind if we borrow your rail cart, do you?"

"You go right ahead Chinaman," Mick said. "But you won't be pulling that cart for long. I guarantee it!"

Li and Shen finished their water and then went over and moved their bags and tools onto the front cart.

"When it gets dark, the race stops till morning, right?" Mick proclaimed.

"There was never any discussion about that, Mick," Li stated firmly.

"The hell you say!" Mick yelled back. "That's why we waited till this morning to start."

"We agreed to start at sunrise, Mick. Nothing was ever said about stopping for dark after the race started," Li reiterated. "'First team into town wins.' Those were your words."

Li and Shen put on their gloves and resumed setting spikes onto the right-side rails using the front rail cart. Mick and Ross continued to blast out profanities toward the Chinamen until they were no longer in sight. Li and Shen regained their pace and never looked back to see where the competition was. Li could tell the Irishmen were exhausted, and he knew that once they lost the lead, they would lose their motivation, and the race would essentially be over.

The afternoon wore on slowly as the Chinamen maintained their steady and monotonous pace. The men spent less and less time looking backward at their competition, and more time looking forward to seeing signs of Reno. Shen continued to ask Li if he wanted to trade positions on the line, and Li continued to decline the offer, even as fatigue increasingly became a factor.

Shen was several rails ahead of Li when he heard a loud screech of pain behind him. He immediately dropped his hammer and ran back to find Li lying on the ground next to the tracks.

"What happened?" Shen shouted.

Li could barely talk. "The sledge hit my ankle."

Shen quickly knelt and untied Li's boot to gain a view of his ankle. The ankle was already swollen to almost twice its normal size.

"Is it bleeding?" Li asked.

"No," said Shen. "But it is swelling up fast."

"Leave the boot on!" Li groaned. "It will help the swelling." Li fell to his back on the ground, wailing in pain.

"What can I do?" Shen asked, feeling helpless and scared.

"Just a moment," Li said under his breath. As he lay on the ground with his eyes closed, he fell into a trance-like state, breathing deliberately and repeatedly in through his nose and out through his mouth.

Shen paced back and forth, waiting for Li to gain control of his pain. After several minutes, Li let out one last breath and opened his eyes. Shen knelt beside him and wiped the sweat from Li's forehead.

"Can you sit up and take a drink?" Shen asked. Li raised his head and lifted himself to his elbows. Shen placed a bedroll under Li's shoulders to support him and offered him the cup of water. Li took a drink and then closed eyes again and rested for a few more minutes.

"I need to get up and walk," Li whispered with his eyes still closed.

"Okay," said Shen hesitantly. "What do you want me to do?"

"Tie my boot as tight as you can," he said. "And then help me up."

Shen tightened the boot around Li's swollen ankle and lifted him onto his feet. Li slowly let go of Shen's grasp and took a few steps on his own. The pain in his ankle was excruciating. But he knew that it was only going to get worse once the shock-induced adrenaline wore off. He took a few more steps and then turned around and walked back to Shen.

"I think it will be okay, as long as I keep moving," Li said, trying to regain confidence in Shen and himself. "You are going to have to swing the sledge," he told Shen. "Are you ready?"

"Yes. Of course, Li," replied Shen. "Whatever you need me to do."

"The sun will be down soon," Li said. "We must both stay alert to our activity to avoid another accident."

"Yes, of course," Shen repeated nervously.

"I will be fine, my friend," Li said compassionately, sensing the fear in Shen's voice. They both exchanged smiles before grabbing their gloves and going back to work.

It was dark when Li and Shen finally saw the lights of Reno below them. It had been a long and grueling day, and the Chinamen were too exhausted to be cheerful about their accomplishment. Li set the last spike on the rail just outside of the junction and then sat down on the tracks to wait for Shen. When Shen secured the last spike, he dropped the sledgehammer and went over to sit next to his friend. The two men hugged in silence for a few moments, and then Li put his hands on Shen's shoulders and looked him in the eyes.

"I am so proud of you, Shen. You showed tremendous strength and character today," he said with sincere relief.

"Oh, dear Li. You taught me something about myself today that I will remember forever," Shen replied with tears in his eyes and then embraced his friend once more.

"Now, I think we need to find a doctor," Li said, bringing them both back to reality.

"Yes. Of course. You stay right here," Shen said as he stood up and walked briskly into town to find help.

Shen returned a few minutes later with Dr. Will, who helped escort the patient to his office. The doctor removed the boot and looked closely at Li's injured ankle.

"This may take a while," Dr. Will stated as he looked over at Shen sitting in the corner. "I think it's best if Li stays here tonight."

"Yes, I understand," said Shen, as he stood and walked to the door. "I will go and find Paddy and the rest of the crew."

"Shen," Li said. "Don't forget the canvas bag on the cart. I will catch up with you in the morning."

Shen flashed his bright smile back at Li once more as he walked out the door.

Paddy and the rest of the crew had set camp in one of the long boxcars just outside the station. Shen set his bags on one of the vacant bunkbeds and set Li's bags on the bed next to his.

Paddy was sitting at the table having supper with some of the other foremen.

"Well, well! Looks like the spikers are rolling in," Paddy said as he stood up and walked over to Shen. "Good to see you, Shen. Where are the rest of the boys?"

Shen updated Paddy on the current status of the team as best he could, and then went over to the stove and spooned out some rice.

"Hell of a job today, Shen!" Paddy said out loud so that everyone else could hear. "I'll check on Li in the morning. You get some sleep."

By the time Mick and Ross reached the town and found the boxcar, Shen was asleep in his bed. Mick nudged him with his boot. "Where's Li?"

Shen rolled over and explained what had happened to Li.

"Well, if that ain't the bloody shits, I don't know what is!" Mick blurted out as he staggered away. The Irishmen unloaded their gear and went directly to the saloon.

Mick and Ross returned later that night and waited outside until the rest of the crew had left the boxcar. They walked in quietly and locked the door behind them. Once they knew they were alone, Mick rushed over to Shen's bedside, grabbed a pillow and smothered it over his face. Shen awoke and started shaking and kicking violently. "Hold his legs down!" Mick whispered quickly to Ross. Ross grabbed Shen's legs as tight as he could, and then lay down on top of Shen. Mick forced the pillow against Shen's face with one arm and reached under the pillow and choked his throat as hard as he could with his other hand. Finally, after a valiant fight by Shen, the resistance in the Chinaman's body ceased and everything fell into stillness.

Li was awake and finishing breakfast in bed when Dr. Will came in. Paddy and Jesse also walked in behind the doctor.

"Good morning, Li," said Dr. Will as he removed the breakfast tray from Li's lap. "How did you sleep?"

"Very well, thank you," he replied.

The doctor pulled back the blanket at the foot of the bed to reveal Li's injured ankle. Paddy and Jesse approached the bed to get a look at the injury.

"You had quite the day yesterday!" exclaimed Paddy. I am truly impressed that you managed to complete that section of track in one day, especially with that ankle," pointing to the painfully swollen and bruised foot.

"Shen and I both put in a hard day," replied Li.

The standing men all glanced at each other in a moment of uncomfortable silence before Jesse finally spoke.

"Son, we have some bad news about Shen. We found him in his bed this morning. But he was not alive when we found him."

The room fell silent, allowing Li to process the news. Li, stunned beyond words, sat silently, and stared out the window to the side of the bed. His breathing became shallow and unsteady, and his skin became cold and clammy. Feelings were stirring inside his chest that he had never felt before. His hands curled into tight fists, as he visualized his friend's condition.

"Li," said Jesse. "I know this is a difficult time. But is there anything that might have happened to Shen yesterday on the track that could have led to his death?"

Li took a few more moments to gain control over his breathing before responding to the question.

"Was there a canvas bag of money inside Shen's belongings?" Li asked suggestively.

Jesse looked at Paddy and they both shook their heads.

"No, there wasn't," replied Jesse. "Why do you ask?"

Li proceeded to tell the men in the room about the events over the last couple of days. The three men listened closely to Li's story, including his conclusions regarding the death of Shen and the probable location of the canvas bag. The men could feel the silent rage that was smoldering inside of Li.

"Li, thank you for helping us better understand this situation," Jesse said. "We'll let you get some rest while we step outside and discuss this further."

After some further discussion, the three men agreed on how to proceed with the situation at hand. Jesse and Paddy walked out of the doctor's office together, while Dr. Will stayed behind.

Goddamnit!" Jesse yelled out in anger as they walked outside onto the street. "I don't have to live with those bastards, law or no law!" He paused to gather his thoughts, and then looked directly into Paddy's eyes. "You listen to me Paddy," he said with a serious tone in his voice. "Either you get rid of those God-damned fools, or I will get rid of all of you! Understood?"

The doctor returned to Li's room and proceeded to inspect the injured ankle. When there was no discussion regarding Shen's death, Li initiated the conversation.

"Dr. Will, did you inspect Shen after his death?" asked Li.

"Yes, Li. I did," replied Dr. Will.

"Was there any sign of violence?"

"His neck was scratched and bruised. But that's all."

"So, he was strangled," Li concluded.

"Perhaps, but probably not conclusive," replied Dr. Will. "Listen to me, son. Reno is a small town, a long way from just about everything," the doctor said as he sat down on the side of the bed. "And with all the changes coming out this way, it sometimes gets hard to separate right from wrong," the doctor waited a moment to see if Li understood. "Sometimes it's best to leave things alone and move on with our lives, to avoid making things even worse. Does that make sense, Li?"

"Does it make sense to you, Dr. Will?" Li replied.

The doctor thought for a moment, "No, I guess not," he conceded, as he stood up to leave. "But right or wrong, you need to look out for yourself. You understand?" Dr. Will patted Li on the leg and then walked out of the room.

Li was resting on the front porch of the doctor's office when Jesse walked up with another man.

"How are you feeling, Li?" Jesse asked.

"Much better, thank you."

"I want you to meet Mr. Charles Taylor, a U.S. Senator from Oregon."

"How do you do, Li?" the senator greeted Li with a handshake.

"Fine, sir, thank you."

"Jesse tells me you are one of his best workers. At least when you're healthy," said the senator pointing to Li's ankle.

"I will be fine in a day or two, sir."

"That's good because I have been asked by the president to bring back some hard-working Chinamen to help out around the White House. Does that interest you, Li?"

Li looked over at Jesse.

"It's better pay and cleaner work, Li," said Jesse. "I wouldn't let you go if I didn't think it was best for you."

Li thought about the offer for a moment. "I am very grateful to both of you for the opportunity. I look forward to working for the president," Li responded.

"That's great!" exclaimed the senator. "Will you be able to travel by Friday?"

"I will be fine by Friday, sir."

"Terrific. We will see you at the station first thing Friday morning," The senator said as he tipped his hat and departed.

Jesse stood at the edge of the porch watching the senator walk away, and thinking of what to say to Li.

"Li," he began. "I know this doesn't make everything right. But it is a good opportunity for you, and probably the best solution for everyone."

"Maybe so," Li replied. "But I cannot help but feel responsible for Shen's death. It fills my heart with sorrow."

"Well, son," said Jesse. "It's not your fault. It's this damn country! Everyone is running around like chickens with their heads cut off! There is just no common sense anymore; no respect for each other."

Li could tell that Jesse was hurting inside also.

"In my country," Li stated quietly. "It is believed that self-indulgence always comes with a consequence. And, likewise, a world of conflict and suffering is an opportunity for one to achieve great peace of mind through empathy and compassion."

Jesse looked at Li and smiled. "That's funny. My momma used to say, '*At the end of the day, we all have to accept our actions and live with the consequences.*'"

Li smiled back at Jesse. "Maybe we are not so different after all."

CHAPTER SEVEN

The caravan leaving Reno consisted of one stagecoach carrying the senator and a small entourage, one Wells Fargo stagecoach carrying bank deposits and payloads, and three covered wagons carrying cooking and camping supplies along with a few second-class passengers, including Li. There were also several men on horseback, hired to safely escort the caravan through Indian territory. The senator's party was scheduled to take the caravan into Omaha, Nebraska, where they would then board the Union Pacific Railroad System into Washington, DC.

Arriving in Omaha was a welcome sight for the senator's party, as that meant the end of a long and dusty wagon ride. Furthermore, Omaha was a small but vibrant community located on the edge of the American frontier. The town was established on the west bank of the Missouri River soon after the ferry was installed, creating the only connection between the east and west banks of the river. Known as the "Gateway to the West," Omaha became the crossroads for the westbound pioneers, trappers, prospectors, cattle ranchers, and railroad industrialists.

The party arrived at the station and unloaded their belongings. One of the senator's aides came back to the covered wagon and communicated the plan for the next few days. Li and a couple of Chinamen were directed to one of the local hotels where they could stay at a reasonable rate. The men were told to rest up and enjoy themselves for the next two days and be at the train station by 9 a.m. on Sunday for the train's departure to Washington, DC.

Li checked into his room and immediately lay down for a long and welcome nap on a soft bed. Li's room was located on the second floor, behind the main hotel. His room had access to an outdoor staircase leading to the bathhouse, and to a second-floor balcony connecting to the main hotel and saloon. Following his nap, Li washed up and went into town to have supper. After supper, he walked casually around town looking at the shops and businesses along the main street. He found the town very clean and accommodating and the people to be very cordial. There was a positive energy about Omaha. Everyone seemed to have a purpose for being in Omaha and they were excited about their future. When he returned to his hotel room, the adjacent saloon had become quite busy. From his room, he could hear the voices in the saloon competing with the loud and festive piano music below him.

Li closed the door to his room and lay down on his bed

to read. After a couple of hours of reading and quiet meditation, he walked back down to the bathhouse to relieve himself before retiring for the night. As he walked downstairs, he heard a loud scream, followed by a man yelling profanities. He could tell the voices were coming from the main hotel adjacent to his balcony. He paused on the staircase to look over at the hotel. It was then that he saw the shadow of a man through the back window of one of the hotel rooms. He heard the screaming noise again and was convinced that it was the scream of a distressed woman in the room with the man. Li walked quickly down the outdoor balcony and entered the hotel hallway from the back. He suddenly found himself on the second floor of the main hotel, overlooking the loud and raucous saloon. He proceeded down the hallway to the distressed woman's room. He paused for a moment to listen for the voices again, but the saloon below him was all he could hear. He concluded that he had no choice but to knock on the door.

The door opened halfway and stopped. A woman stood behind the door while leaning her head around to speak to Li. All he could see was her tangled hair hanging down her face and her tearful eyes.

"Pardon me, madam. I thought I heard some yelling from outside. Is everything all right?" Li asked.

"Oh, um, yes," replied the woman. "Everything is fine."

The woman was crying and visibly harmed physically

and emotionally. Li tried to think of something else to say before she closed the door. Suddenly, he saw a stream of blood come out from her nostrils and run down her chin onto the floor.

"Are you sure everything is all right, madam?" Li pleaded again.

Suddenly, the door swung fully open and the woman was pulled violently onto the bed from behind. In her place stood a half-dressed man in a rage of anger.

"Did you not hear what the woman said!" yelled the man. "Now, get the hell out of here," he said.

"I am sorry, sir, but the lady seems to be hurt and needs help," Li said as he tried to look around the man in the doorway.

"The woman is fine," the man yelled, "but you are about to get beat to hell." The man stepped quickly through the doorway toward Li and reached out and shoved Li viciously across the hallway. Li reacted instinctively to the assault by grabbing the man's extended arm with both hands while rotating his body into the man and lifting him over his back. The momentum of the man's assault launched him over the handrail behind Li and toward the saloon below. Li held on tight to the man's arm with both hands, as the man swung down and crashed against the outside of the banister, leaving him hanging helplessly above the crowded saloon.

"Help me!" cried the man looking up at Li. "Oh, God, please don't let me fall!"

The saloon patrons gasped and then fell silent, as the man swung over them. Everyone quickly evacuated the tables underneath the dangling man, while some women screamed in horror as they ran away from danger.

Li was straining to keep his grip on the man. He leaned back to help stabilize his hold. "Grab the rail," Li yelled to the man. "Grab the rail."

The man reached up and took hold of the handrail with his free hand. Li let loose with one of his hands and quickly reached over the railing and grabbed the man's other wrist. Then he leaned back and pulled as hard as he could, lifting the man up until he was hanging over the top of the banister and eventually tumbling on top of Li as they both collapsed onto the hallway floor.

One of the bartenders rushed up the stairs.

"Are you all right?" asked the bartender, looking at the two men lying in the hallway.

Li stood up and looked over the condition of the man on the floor.

"Yes. I think we are all fine now," replied Li.

"You scared us all half to death!" exclaimed the bartender. "Shall I call the doctor?" he asked. "Or the sheriff?"

"No," yelled the man as he lifted himself off the floor. "Just leave us alone!"

Li walked into the room to find the woman sitting on the bed, filled with fear and disbelief. The man walked in behind Li and closed the door.

The man proceeded to get dressed while continuing to threaten Li. From the appearance of his clothes, he was obviously a very wealthy man.

"Do you know who I am," the man said belligerently. "I could have you put in jail until hell freezes over!"

Li did not reply to the man's rage but stood silently in the corner of the room next to the battered woman sitting on the bed.

"You go right ahead and call the sheriff, Nathan," the woman yelled back at the man. "I'll have him put you away, you bastard. You can't treat me like that and get away with it. I don't care who you think you are!"

The man finished dressing and reached down to grab a money pouch lying on the table next to Li. Li quickly rested his hand on the table in front of the money.

"Leave the pouch," Li stated calmly. "I believe it belongs to the lady now."

There was a tense pause as the two men locked eyes. Li waited for the man to respond. The man stood back from the table and thought about his next move. As angry as he was, he realized that he was in no position to win this argument and eventually gave up and turned away from the bag on the table.

"To hell with the both of you!" he said as he walked out of the room and slammed the door behind him.

Li let out a sigh of relief, as he stood in the corner trying to replay in his head what had just happened. The woman stood up, still showing anger, and walked over to look at her wounds in the mirror. She was young—maybe twenty-five or thirty years old—with long dark hair, dark eyes, and soft pale skin. She was dressed quite suggestively, but her posture and the tone of her voice indicated a more conservative nature.

She tried to clean the blood off her face and brush her hair back into place before she turned around and faced Li. Li suddenly felt very awkward and out of place.

"I'm sorry you had to be part of all that," she said. "But I'm also glad you showed up when you did. I can usually see it coming, but boy did I miss that one," she said as she laughed nervously and wiped the tears from her eyes.

Li started to move toward the door.

"What's your name?" she asked.

"Li."

"I'm Rose," she said as she attempted a polite smile.

They both stood quietly for a few moments, letting their emotions settle. When the awkward feeling returned to the room, Li started toward the door again.

"Thank you," Rose said quietly and sincerely.

"You are welcome, Rose. I hope you find comfort soon." Li said as he turned and walked out the door.

As Li walked down the hallway, Rose stepped out of the room.

"Li, wait," she hollered from the doorway. "I feel like I should repay you in some way. How about you come to the house tomorrow night, and I will cook dinner?"

Li thought for a moment, then smiled and nodded his

head.

"I live at 'Prairie Rose' south of town, just past the cemetery."

Li nodded again and waved, then returned to his room.

Li walked to the edge of town where he found a small cemetery on a gentle hillside. From the cemetery, Li could see grasslands extending endlessly into the darkening horizon. To the east, he saw the vast prairie give way to the Missouri River, lined on both sides with tall deciduous trees and giving life to everything it touched as it meandered across the countryside. Just beyond the cemetery, Li came to a private drive with beautiful pink rose bushes on both sides and an arch over the entrance that read "Prairie Rose."

"Hello, Li," Rose said as she opened the front door. "I'm so glad you came."

"Thank you for the kind invitation."

"Please, come in and make yourself comfortable."

Li walked into the small house and closed the door behind him. Inside, he could see a small kitchen at one end of the house, and a small living area centered around a wood-burning fireplace at the other end. There was a wooden dining table sitting in the middle of the room, with three table settings and a vase of wildflowers in the middle. A wooden ladder rested against the loft above the kitchen, which led to the sleeping quarters.

"Cooper," Rose said as she walked back into the

kitchen, "come down and meet Mr. Li."

After a moment, a young boy glanced over the loft at Li, and then turned around and backed down the ladder one step at a time. When he reached the bottom, he turned around and extended his hand.

"Hi. My name is Cooper."

"Hello, Cooper. My name is Li," Li said, as he reached out and shook Cooper's hand.

"How old are you, Cooper?"

"Six. But I can ride a horse all by myself," he stated confidently.

"Is that right? You sound like a very responsible young man."

"Okay, let's eat," Rose announced from the kitchen.

Cooper ran over and quickly sat down at the table. Li followed him to the table and then waited for Rose before seating himself.

"Please, sit down, Li," Rose said. "We're not that formal around here."

"Thank you," Li said and took a seat next to Cooper.

"Hope you like beans," Rose said as she placed a cast-iron pot in the middle of the table and handed Li a large spoon. "Help yourself." Rose returned to the kitchen and removed a pan of cornbread from the oven and then joined the others at the table.

After dinner, Cooper cleared off the table and rinsed the plates before returning to his loft. Li and Rose moved over to a small couch facing the warm fire and sat quietly, drinking their coffee.

"Are you feeling better today?" Li asked Rose.

"Yes, I feel better," she replied. "Still sore and angry, though."

"Yes, well the soreness will go away with time," Li said. "The anger is a reaction to the way you were treated and will go away whenever you decide."

"So, how do I make it go away?" Rose asked curiously.

"By allowing your mind to let go of the past and redirect your thoughts to something more positive. Positive thoughts lead to positive actions," Li stated.

Rose looked at Li with a confused face.

"I know," Li replied with a shrug and a smile. "But it is the answer to your question."

"Well, in the meantime," said Rose. "That pouch he left had a lot of money in it. And I want to share it with you."

"Thank you, Rose, but that money will do more good in your hands than in mine."

"But surely you can use some additional money," exclaimed Rose.

"Honestly, Rose, I have very few needs and more than enough money to meet those needs. I would be much happier seeing that money put to use helping you and your family."

Rose thanked Li for his generosity, as they both sat quietly staring at the fire and drinking their coffee.

"May I ask about Cooper's father?" Li said.

"That would be Daniel," Rose replied. "He died about

a year ago. He got drafted into the war soon after we moved out here and never returned."

"I am so sorry to hear that."

"Yeah, he was a good man," she reminisced. "He brought me out here from Pennsylvania. He kept telling me, *'This is the future!'* He knew the Homestead Act would change everything out West, and he wanted to be a part of the new frontier. We had big plans, but they just never had a chance to come about."

"I have no doubt he was a very good man," Li said.

"What about you, Li. How did you find your way to Omaha?"

"Well," Li paused and considered how much detail to offer. "I started in San Francisco working on the railroad. When we got to Nevada, I was asked to go to Washington, DC, and work at the White House. We stopped in Omaha for a few days to transfer onto a train."

"So, you're leaving soon?" Rose asked.

"Tomorrow morning."

The conversation continued casually into the evening until the fireplace flames had burned to glowing embers.

Rose finished her coffee and set the cup on the hearth. She then slid across the couch next to Li, took his cup and set it on the hearth, and then snuggled up close, caressing his lap, while kissing him on the neck. Li's body trembled with excitement. He closed his eyes and let his head relax into the sofa. Rose parted her blouse and enfolded her bare breasts firmly against him. Li felt as if he was falling from the sky and could not catch himself. Suddenly, he opened his eyes and tried to regain his composure. He withdrew from Rose's embrace and leaned forward putting his hands on his knees.

"Is it because I am a prostitute?" Rose asked as she slid back away from Li.

"No, absolutely not," Li replied quickly as he looked into her eyes.

They both sat quietly until the awkward moment had diminished somewhat.

"I didn't come out here to be a whore, you know," Rose stated as she began to cry. "When Daniel died, it was just me and Cooper. I had no idea what to do. I sold all the cattle, the pigs, chickens—everything—just to stay alive. Then I started getting ranchers coming out wanting to buy our farm. I couldn't do that, so I went to work. This was never how it was supposed to be." Rose stood and walked over to the dining table, where she grabbed a napkin and wiped her tears.

"You have done a noble thing in providing for your son," Li said. "I can only imagine the suffering you have overcome."

Li tried desperately to find the words he wanted to say, but his mind was conflicted. Rose and Li sat on the couch in peaceful silence for a while longer.

"I should go," Li finally whispered as he stood.

"I'm sorry I made you uncomfortable, Li," Rose said.

"No, do not apologize. I am sorry I could not be more

helpful to you."

Rose opened the door and they both walked out onto the porch.

"Thank you for the dinner," Li said. "You have a wonderful home and a wonderful son."

Rose embraced Li with a genuine heartfelt hug and then watched as he walked through the gate and onto the road toward town. "You're always welcome here, Li," Rose hollered from the front door.

Li smiled back at Rose and waved one more time.

CHAPTER EIGHT

The train from Omaha to Washington, DC, was a welcome change from the long and bumpy stagecoach. Plus, it provided Li with another opportunity to enjoy the experience of a train ride. When the train arrived at the DC station, there was a horse-drawn carriage waiting for Senator Taylor. The coachman greeted Mr. Taylor and took his baggage to the back of the carriage.

"These two gentlemen will be accompanying me to the White House," said the senator pointing to Li and another Chinaman.

"Very well, sir," the coachman replied and then loaded the baggage from the Chinamen as well.

After a short trip through town, the stagecoach arrived at a boarding house near the capitol.

"This is my stop gentlemen," the senator said as he stepped out of the coach. "The driver will take you to the servants' quarters at the White House. I hope you enjoy your new jobs."

A few minutes later, the stagecoach pulled through the

White House gates and down a long, tree-lined, and perfectly maintained road to the back of the White House. The two men exited the coach, grabbed their bags, and were escorted through the back doors and into the White House basement, where they met a tall Black gentleman dressed in a butler's uniform.

"Good evening, gentlemen," the man said. "My name is William, and I will show you to your living quarters."

The following morning, Li was taken to a large glass-framed shed, where he was introduced to Oliver Jackson, the White House gardener.

"Welcome to the White House greenhouse," Oliver said with juvenile humor. "Have you ever worked in a garden, Li?"

"Yes, sir, I have. But I look forward to your guidance."

"Well, my first guidance is to make you aware that Mrs. Lincoln is an avid gardener and will frequently visit the conservatory and participate in caring for the plants. You will address her as 'Mrs. President' until she tells you otherwise, and you will never disagree with her suggestions. Understood?"

"Yes, of course," replied Li.

"Okay, let's get to work," said Oliver.

Oliver was a lean and strong young man. He came to the White House as a freed slave after his aunt became the seamstress for Mrs. Lincoln. He was a jovial fellow but always followed the rules and never questioned 'why.' Because of this discipline, he had been allowed great freedom within the conservatory.

Li settled into a daily routine at the White House and had become especially accustomed to the regular meals, soft beds and frequent baths. One morning he was tilling a garden on the White House grounds when Mrs. Lincoln wandered by.

"Good morning, Li," she said with a tone of despair.

"Good morning, Mrs. Lincoln," Li replied cordially.

"Oh, Li. You always have such a nice expression in your voice," she said, trying to find the right words. "Sort of like contentment, or appreciation, or something."

"Thank you, madam. I am grateful for such a compliment."

Li watched her stroll aimlessly around the gardens as if she was looking for some salvation.

"May I help you with anything today, Mrs. Lincoln?"

"No, thank you, Li. I just enjoy being in the gardens. Everything is so fresh and alive."

Li continued with his gardening, while still paying close attention to the president's wife.

"It just seems like the air inside the house has become stale," she acknowledged as she circled back toward Li. "Everyone is so consumed by this wretched war. And the constant news about the mounting death toll is just sucking the life out of the house."

Li continued to listen intently, allowing Mrs. Lincoln to stroll as she pleased.

Just then, an idea came to Li. "Perhaps we could bring some live plants into the house," Li proposed. "Instead of keeping all the plants in the conservatory, they could be placed inside the house, next to windows. We could just as easily care for them inside the house."

"Oh, what a marvelous idea!" exclaimed Mrs. Lincoln. The idea of live plants indoors immediately lifted her spirits. "Please start as soon as possible, can you?"

"She told you to do what?" exclaimed Oliver upon hearing the news from Li.

"Bring live plants into the White House," Li repeated.

"Just how do you propose we do that, Li?"

"We can make smaller pots, filled with soil and starter shoots from our conservatory."

"Oh, Lord!" Oliver sighed. "And now we gotta spend all day inside the White House watering, trimming, and cleaning out the dead plants."

"Perhaps, but I was told to never disagree with the president's wife," Li replied with an indisputable smile.

Li immediately began bringing beautiful live flowering plants into the White House. And it seemed the more plants he brought in the more Mrs. Lincoln wanted. Soon, there were plants of all sorts spread throughout the halls and rooms in the White House. As frustrated as it made Oliver, he could not deny how pleased it made Mrs. Lincoln. Li now spent more time inside the White House, maintaining the house plants.

"You must be Li," said the president as he walked out of his office and found Li watering a plant in the hallway.

"Yes, Mr. President. I am Li."

"Well, I knew that because of the way my wife speaks of you lately. She has become quite fond of you, Li, and simply loves having all these fresh plants in her home."

"Oh, thank you, sir. I am most grateful for the opportunity to work for you and Mrs. Lincoln." Li replied.

"I must admit, I have come to enjoy the plants as well," said the president. "Keep up the good work, son," he said as he resumed his walk down the hall.

Living in the servant's quarters of the White House allowed Li to engage with the other servants and learn a great deal about their lives in America. Even though the Black servants he lived with were free citizens, they still harbored painful memories from their past.

"Oh, Lord," exclaimed Oliver when asked about his past experiences. "I got separated from my mother when I was just a boy. I still don't know where my father is. I watched them drag him away after he was sold in an auction. Me and my brother was left alone when I was ten years old. We worked in the cotton fields for a white man farmer for years until my brother was killed in a knife fight one night. After that, I got moved around a lot. My aunt found me and brought me here. She knows where my momma is too, and we are trying desperately to get her freed."

Li was so taken back by the story; he could hardly believe what he was hearing. And the casual tone in Oliver's voice as he described such a horrific tale made the story seem even more outrageous. Li looked closer into Oliver's eyes, expecting to see the anger and the pain of his losses. Instead, he saw the gratitude of a man who has been saved and the stoic resilience of a patient soul.

"Do you think there will ever be an end to slavery?" he asked.

"Well, now that we have been emancipated, we at least have a path to freedom for all the slaves," Oliver replied. "I am hopeful that will allow us to all be together again soon."

Li was tending to the indoor plants in the president's office one evening when the president walked in.

"Oh, hello, Li," said Mr. President. "Please, keep doing your chores. I just came in for some quiet time."

"Thank you, sir," replied Li. "I will not be long."

Li continued tending to the house plants, while President Lincoln sat in his desk chair looking out the window behind his desk.

"Li, may I ask you something?"

"Of course, Mr. President."

"I am not trying to pry, mind you," he said as he turned his chair around. "But you interact with the Black servants enough to have a valued perspective. I am interested in their thoughts on the war, and how they see the war impacting their lives."

Li thought for a moment, trying to formulate a truthful response.

"Well, sir, from what I understand, many of the Black servants have suffered tremendously, both personally and as a community, over the last several years. Their constant physical torture and mental strife have been so overwhelming, there was little hope left in their lives. However, their hopes and aspirations have been greatly renewed by the recent Emancipation Proclamation."

"Yes," replied the president. "I wish we would have done that a long time ago. But, more specifically, do they think their lives will be impacted by the outcome of the war?"

"Again, sir," stated Li. "It is my understanding from conversations with my coworkers that they think the war is less about slavery and more about keeping the states under a single union."

"Yes, that is what I feared," the President said despondently as he swung his chair around again and resumed looking out the window.

Li finished his duties tending to the plants and gathered his tools to leave. He was on his way out when the president turned around once again.

"What would your leader do about this war, Li?" the President began. "What would your leader do if your country was in a civil war, and over 500,000 fellow countrymen had already been killed?"

Li was completely stunned by the question. His legs weakened and his palms became sweaty as he tried to grasp the magnitude of the president's question. Even though he had thought often about his country being invaded by foreign interests, and how his community would—or should—respond, he never thought about so much death and suffering by his people.

"Sir," Li said with sincerity. "I can only begin to conceive the emotional agony that you are enduring. You see, my country is founded on very sound moral principles, and it is highly unlikely that we would experience such a conflict within our borders." Li paused for a moment, knowing that he had not yet answered the question. "However, I think anyone who has suffered such losses, especially an honorable leader, would be dedicated to ending the conflict in a way that ensures those men did not die in vain."

Li looked at the president for a response. The president remained seated at his desk in deep contemplation. Li quietly picked up his tools and started to leave the room.

"Li," said Mr. Lincoln. "What is the name of your country?"

"Tibet, sir."

"Tibet sounds like a wonderful country filled with wonderful people."

"Thank you, sir," Li replied, and then turned and left the President alone in his office.

Li returned to his quarters and lay down on his bed

and tried to rest. He could not stop thinking of President Lincoln and the immense responsibility that he shouldered. His integrity as a man and a president was unquestioned, yet he was facing a situation that was sure to compromise that integrity, regardless of his decision. Li thought about what he would do in such a situation. The thought was so extreme to Li, he simply could not formulate a cohesive solution, and he became filled with anxiety and sadness. He continued to struggle internally with the tremendous burden placed on the president and the horrible images of war until he finally drifted off to sleep.

In a dream-state, Li found himself in the dark of night soaring high above the ground. He heard voices all around him, but could not see anyone, and could not understand any of the words being said. As he soared closer to the ground, the voices became louder and he began to see bodies strewn across the land in every direction. Off in the distance, Li could see a cliff where the mass of bodies appeared to be falling over the edge. When he reached the cliff's edge, Li could see the bottomless chasm and the final destination for the mass of bodies. Suddenly, the loud screaming stopped, the bodies all disappeared, and Li fell, helplessly, over the edge into total darkness. Li then jolted out of his dream and thrust upright in his bed. Sitting on the edge of his bed, he wiped the sweat from his face and tried to settle his racing heart and regain his breath. When his body had recovered, he collapsed back into his bed and fell into a restful state of sleep for the remainder of the night.

With the coming of spring, the trees began to blossom, and the soil was once again warm enough to plant the numerous gardens on the White House grounds. Li was busy planting roses in one of the gardens, when his thoughts drifted back to Omaha, and more specifically, to the Prairie Rose. This was not the first time his thoughts were clouded by Rose. The truth was Li thought about Rose quite often. His heart pained for her in ways he had never felt before. Normally, his mindfulness training was able to overcome such thoughts, but when it came to Rose, he was rendered powerless.

After a prolonged moment of daydreaming, Li regained his presence, only to look up and see Mrs. Lincoln standing next to him in the garden.

"My goodness, Li," Mrs. Lincoln proclaimed. "You look like you were in another world."

"I am sorry, Mrs. Lincoln. My mind was wandering for a moment."

"Perhaps you miss your family back home. That is quite understandable," she replied.

"Actually," Li said with a guilty grin. "It is a young woman I met in Omaha."

"Oh, that makes sense. Nothing clouds a sound mind like a new love."

"You are probably right, but it is only temporary."

"Exactly," exclaimed Mrs. Lincoln. "That is why you must act on those feelings. True love is a rare jewel in life, Li, and any opportunity to discover it must be explored."

CHAPTER NINE

Those encouraging words from Mrs. Lincoln were enough to put Li back on the train to Omaha. After some genuine heartfelt goodbyes to his White House friends, Li found himself once again on his way to a new frontier. The train pulled into Omaha just before sunset. Li checked himself into the hotel and then walked around front to the saloon for dinner. While having dinner, he glanced casually around the saloon and the upstairs hallway, hoping to see Rose. Li finished his dinner and spent the rest of the evening walking around town until it was dark, at which time he retired to his hotel room for the night.

The following morning, Li cleaned himself up in the bathhouse and decided to pay a visit to Rose. As he walked through the gate to the Prairie Rose, he saw both Rose and Cooper walking out of the barn.

"Look, Ma, it's Mr. Li," shouted Cooper.

"Well, what do you know! It sure is," said Rose, as she handed a basket of fresh eggs to Cooper. "Here darling, take this inside and I'll make us some breakfast in a bit."

Rose walked down to the gate and gave Li a big hug and a warm smile. "What a wonderful surprise," she said.

"It is good to see you too, Rose."

"Come on in, Li. You're just in time for breakfast."

"You remember Cooper?" Rose asked as they walked into the house.

"Of course. How are you, Cooper?"

"Fine. Thank you, sir," Cooper said.

"So, tell me what you've been up to, Li," said Rose as she prepared some ham and eggs for breakfast.

"Well, I have been in Washington, DC, working at the White House."

"No, kidding!" exclaimed Rose. "Did you meet the president?"

"Yes, I actually got acquainted with both Mr. and Mrs. Lincoln," replied Li. "Mrs. Lincoln kept me busy tending to all her live plants in the White House."

"Oh my goodness. Were they nice to you?"

"Yes, of course. They are both very kind people.

"That is wonderful," said Rose as she handed everyone their breakfast and then sat down herself.

"How have you been, Rose?" asked Li. "I stayed at the hotel last night and thought I might see you there."

"Well," said Rose. "There have been a lot of changes since you left. Do you remember what you said to me about how to deal with my anger? You told me the anger would go away when I started thinking more positively. Well, I thought about that a lot. Then, it just so happened the schoolteacher in town got drafted into the war, and we were left without a teacher for the children. So, I took the money you left me from that night and got my teacher's credentials. So, I am now officially the town's schoolteacher."

"That's terrific," said Li. "I cannot think of a better teacher than you."

"Well, that isn't exactly what the town council thought. It seems they don't take too kindly to letting 'ladies of ill repute' teach their children how to read and write."

"I see," replied Li. "So, how did you convince them otherwise?"

"I went ahead and got my teacher's credentials, ordered some school supplies, and started recruiting Cooper's friends and classmates. The town tried to find a permanent replacement for a while, but eventually gave up and sent all their kids over to me."

"Very positive thinking," replied Li, shaking his head and smiling.

"That's not all," said Rose. "I asked the town council to build a new schoolhouse since I was teaching out of my house for the past year. They said they had no money to help, so I applied for a government grant and was given $250 to build a new schoolhouse."

"So, it seems good things do happen to good people!" Li replied.

"Apparently it does," Rose concluded. "So, where are you off to next, Li?"

"I have not decided really."

"Well, I could sure use a strong hand around here this summer," Rose said. "I can't offer much more than room and board. But you are more than welcome to stay as long as you like."

"Thank you, Rose. I would enjoy the opportunity to help however I can."

Li decided that it would be best to stay in one of the outbuildings at the Prairie Rose. Over the next couple of days, he was able to modify the loft in the barn to accommodate a straw mattress, a couple of lanterns, and some storage shelves. Once his accommodations were completed, Li worked with Rose on her vision for the schoolhouse. Rose wanted to keep the building designs small and simple, preferring to use any leftover money on schoolbooks and furnishings for the students. Li took the completed design into town and began to order construction materials. He then stopped by the livery stable on his way home.

Cooper was sitting on the front porch when Li rode by the house on a beautiful horse.

"Momma, come look!" yelled Cooper as he ran down and opened the gate for Li.

Rose came out onto the porch and watched as Li rode up to the house and tied the horse to a railing next to the barn.

"What in the world have you done, Li," Rose asked.

"Well, I saw you had a wagon stored behind the barn and thought it would be useful hauling building materials back and forth from town. So, I bought this draft horse from the livery stable to pull the wagon."

"I don't know, Li," said Rose. "That may be more than we can afford right now."

"Well, let's just call it a donation from President Lincoln," Li replied.

Rose smiled and shook her head. "It will come in handy. I'll say that much."

"Cooper, maybe you can help me prepare his stall," Li said as they both walked into the barn.

"What is his name?" asked Cooper.

"His name is Ned, but we can change it if you want."

"No, I like Ned," Cooper concluded after some thought.

The next several days were filled with trips back and forth to town, as the materials for the schoolhouse arrived. Li worked sunup to sundown on the schoolhouse construction. Cooper was interested in the work Li was doing and was more than willing to help when asked. Li took the time to explain as much as he knew about construction to Cooper. In time, Cooper became a helpful resource to Li and they both enjoyed working together.

Li was becoming more comfortable every day and he found himself in a state of happiness that he had never experienced before. He was able to find quiet time in the mornings for meditation, and his evenings were spent enjoying the company of Rose and Cooper and the unique bonds of simple family life. Never had he imagined that his journey would bring him to such a place. He felt guilty at times because he often forgot about his life back in Lhasa. And when he did think of his homeland, it made him confused and conflicted inside. For the first time, Li could see himself staying in America.

Li was sitting on the front porch one evening watching the crescent moon rise over the eastern horizon. Cooper had retreated to his loft, following dinner and a bath, and was reading a book before bed. Rose finished cleaning up the kitchen and walked out onto the porch to sit with Li.

"I am sure that Cooper has reminded you that he has a birthday coming up next week," said Rose as she sat down next to Li. "Lord knows he has reminded me enough times."

"Yes, I have been reminded as well," Li replied with a smile.

"I was thinking that we could host a birthday party and have a schoolhouse raising on the same day since we will have all the families together. Do you think the framing will be ready by then?"

"Yes, that is a wonderful idea. I will make sure everything is ready."

"Thank you, Li," Rose said. "I cannot tell you how grateful I am for your help this summer. I truly do not know what I would have done without you."

Rose slid her hand through Li's arm and snuggled

close while sharing a warm moment together under a beautiful summer sky.

Li spent the rest of the week preparing the walls and trusses for securing. When he had questions, he went into town and spoke with James, the owner of the sawmill, who seemed to know all about barn raisings.

"The raising party is on Saturday," Li said to James. "Is it possible that you could come out and oversee the schoolhouse raising?"

"I don't know, Li," James hesitated. "Is there going to be any food and beer?"

"Absolutely! And there will be a birthday cake for Cooper."

"Well, that's good enough for me. Count me in."

"Great! See you on Saturday."

Li was sitting on the porch just after sunrise, having his morning tea when James arrived with a horse-drawn wagon full of gear.

"Good morning James," Li said as he walked down to open the gate. "I did not expect you this early."

"Well, Li. We take our barn raisings very seriously around here," James said as he rode through the gate. "You best leave the gate open. The rest of the fellas are right behind me."

In no time at all, a dozen men had arrived and were preparing to go to work.

Li rushed inside the house. "Rose, the barn raising

team has arrived! Can you please make some coffee for these men?"

"I'm already on it, Li. And I got some biscuits coming too."

"Thank you," Li said as he returned to the yard.

The men had gathered around James as he unloaded the tools from his wagon and gave out instructions. Once everyone was equipped with tools, James led the men to the schoolhouse and started working.

About an hour into the workday, the gate down by the road opened once again, and another wagon pulled into the yard stacked full of tables and chairs from the church. Behind the wagon was a stream of women and children carrying dishes of food, drinks, and games for the party. Rose greeted the ladies and assisted them in setting up the tables and chairs.

In a matter of minutes, the Prairie Rose was transformed into a well-choreographed festival. The kids were all playing together behind the barn, while the ladies organized the food and refreshments in the front yard and the men engaged in synchronized teamwork assembling the new schoolhouse.

Li was amazed at the kindness and generosity exhibited by these people. It had been so long since he felt truly connected to a community, he had forgotten how warm and comfortable the feeling was. He found himself standing alone by the porch, observing in total reverence while wiping tears of grateful joy from his eyes.

By late afternoon, the men had erected the schoolhouse wall frames and roof trusses and completed the metal roof and most of the outside siding. They even built a small bell tower atop the roof. Rose came out onto the front porch and hollered to the men.

"Okay everybody, it's supper time. Wash your hands in the barn, grab a drink, and find a seat."

The men gradually finished up their work and began cleaning up the site.

"Well, I reckon you and Cooper can finish up from here, Li," James said as he loaded his tools in the wagon. "Any problems, you know where to find me."

"I do not know how I can thank you and these men, James. Your generosity is inspiring, and I am most grateful."

"Well, most of these men had their barns built the same way. I guess what goes around, comes around."

"Then I look forward to returning the favor someday," Li replied.

While the men had been working on the schoolhouse, the women had been busy assembling a delicious assortment of meats, vegetables, and desserts for the evening feast. Everyone filled their plates from the buffet and were seated casually around the tables or on the porch and the front yard.

Rose walked out onto the porch with her glass in hand. "Okay, listen up everybody," she hollered as loud as she could. "I'd liked to say grace before we all dive in."

The party quieted and everyone held hands as Rose began to speak.

"Bless us, O Lord, and these, thy gifts, which we are about to receive. And bless our friends that have come here today to show their generous support for this community. And a special blessing to Li, who has come into our lives and worked selflessly and without judgment and has shown us all the path to grace. Through Christ, our Lord. Amen."

"Amen," replied the party.

"And Happy birthday to Cooper!" yelled one of the parents. Then, everyone sang the birthday song while the kids teased Cooper.

The meal was delicious, and the friendly atmosphere carried on into the night. Everyone gathered around the fire pit, telling stories, and singing songs. Li was washing dishes outside by the horse trough while watching the party settle into peaceful contentment. James had retrieved his guitar from the wagon and was sitting near the fire playing a mix of gospel and country melodies. One song, in particular, captured Li's affection.

> *As I remember, I was just a boy*
> *When Mamma sat with me and told her story*
> *It might have been love, but we were both so young*
> *She said he took my heart but gave me my only son*
>
> *She had no choice but to grow up fast*
> *Her hopes and dreams but a distant past*

Life is hard and not always fair
But there is good and grace most everywhere

She tells me now to be a simple man
Keep an open heart and an open hand
Reach for the stars, but don't take them away
Best leave them there for your son one day

James finished the song with a beautiful acoustical refrain, and then glanced over to Li. Li was standing with his hands together and bowed gently, giving his full blessings to the soulful song and to James. There was a warm connection between the two gentlemen as they both smiled at each other.

The party continued until the fire burned low and the kids finally tired. Li and Rose stood by the gate and thanked everyone for the wonderful party and especially for their contribution to the new schoolhouse. When the last guest had left, Rose and Li turned back toward the house.

"I've been meaning to tell you how beautiful these rose bushes look this time of the year," Li said as he walked through the rose framed gate. "You know, they say pink roses are a sign of joy and happiness."

"I know," Rose replied with a charming smile as she closed the gate behind them.

Rose held Li's hand as they walked back to the house.

"Goodnight, Rose," Li said as he parted from Rose and

turned toward the barn, Rose pulled him back and embraced him with a warm hug and a passionate kiss. The feeling of her soft lips weakened his body, and he willingly melted into her grasp. The exchange finished with a long silent hug before Rose gently withdrew, smiled at Li, and walked into the house.

Li proceeded up to his loft and lay down on his bed and closed his eyes. He was exhausted from the busy day, and yet still stimulated by his encounter with Rose. There were so many reasons to keep a platonic relationship with Rose, including his monastic oath of celibacy as an ordained monk. And yet, he could not stop thinking about her sultry soft body in his embrace, and the feeling of her lips against his. The fact was, he was in love with Rose and wanted to be closer to her in every way possible. He extinguished his lamp, closed his eyes, and tried to go to sleep. After a few minutes, he heard a noise in the barn below the loft. It sounded like footsteps in the dry hay. He lay still, listening when suddenly, Rose appeared on the loft. She moved quietly over to the bed, slipped out of her gown, and pulled herself under the covers next to Li.

The following morning, Li and Rose were sitting at the table having coffee when Cooper awakened and climbed down from his Loft.

"Good morning, sweetheart," said Rose. "Do you feel older today?"

"No, Mom," Cooper replied, refusing to acknowledge the humor.

"Well, I think you look older," stated Rose. "What do you think, Li?"

"Older and smarter," Li replied.

"What do you say we walk over to the barn and get some eggs and I'll cook us up a big birthday breakfast," said Rose as she ruffled her hand through Cooper's hair.

The three of them walked out to the barn. As they opened the barn door and walked in, Cooper stopped and looked closer in the horse stalls.

"Momma, look," he said. "There is another horse in the stall with Ned. It must be someone from the party last night."

"No, Cooper," Rose replied. "That's your birthday present from me and Mr. Li."

Cooper's eyes lit up in disbelief as he ran over and climbed up onto the railing. "Really? I can't believe it! He's beautiful!"

"Can I ride him?" he asked.

"After breakfast," Rose answered quickly. "And only with Mr. Li until you're comfortable by yourself."

Rose continued into the chicken coop to gather eggs, while Cooper and Li stood next to the horse stall.

"What's his name?" asked Cooper.

"Well, this young colt does not have a name yet," replied Li. "That will be up to you to name him whatever you like."

"Wow! I can't wait to ride him."

"Breakfast first, Cooper," said Rose as she emerged

from the chicken coop.

After breakfast, Li and Cooper went back into the barn, where Li taught Cooper how to saddle his horse and lead him outside. Once outside, Li instructed Cooper on all the proper ways to handle and care for a young horse. Once Cooper was comfortable with his horse, Li saddled up Ned and went for a short ride down to the creek with Cooper and his new friend. They dismounted to let the horses drink from the creek and then tied them off to a tree while they sat by the creek for a while and talked.

"How old were you when you learned to ride a horse, Mr. Li," asked Cooper.

"Oh, I guess I was about your age. Maybe eight or nine years old."

"Where did you grow up?" asked Cooper.

"I was born in a small village out in the country, but I grew up in a town called 'Lhasa.'"

"Were there lots of horses there?"

"Yes, we rode horses quite often."

Cooper was in deep thought for a moment. Then he repeated the town a couple of times. "Lhasa. Is that right? Lhasa."

"Yes," replied Li.

"I like that name. Can I name my horse 'Lhasa'?"

"That is a beautiful name for a horse," Li answered.

"Yes, that will be his name," said Cooper as he got up and walked over to his horse. "Your name is Lhasa," he whispered to the horse, and then brushed his hand gently along the horse's neck.

After the horses had been rested, Li and Cooper mounted up and started back toward the house. When they reached the main road, Li saw another man riding toward them. As the man approached, Li recognized him immediately as the man who abused Rose in the saloon that night. The man did not recognize Li at first, but as they got closer and passed each other, the man suddenly remembered. He turned around and looked back at Li, but Li kept riding. While it was obvious that both men recognized each other, neither man chose to acknowledge the other on that day.

That evening, Li and Rose were sitting on the porch after dinner, watching Cooper and a couple of friends play in the yard.

"Rose, what ever happened to that man that beat you in the hotel that night?", Li asked casually.

"You mean Nathan? He's still around. He has a big ranch across the river. Seems the railroad business has made him a rich man."

"Has he ever bothered you again?"

"No, not me anyway. I hear he's hit a couple of other girls though. Beat one girl up so bad, they had to take her to Chicago to get help."

"Why doesn't the sheriff do something?"

"He tries to. But every time the sheriff locks Nathan up, the Mayor comes in and reminds him just how much Nathan contributes to the community. Next thing you know, Nathan is out again."

Li's body became cold and clammy. He began to tremble and could not sit still. He stood up and walked to the edge of the porch. Suddenly, he became lightheaded and dizzy. He quickly grabbed the handrail and leaned against the corner post to steady himself. His face turned pale and sweat beaded on his forehead.

"Are you ok, dear?", Rose asked after seeing him stumble.

"Yes. I am fine now. I think that story took my breath away. I have never felt like that before."

"Maybe you should go lie down for a while. It's getting late anyway."

Rose walked with Li over to the barn. She gave him a big hug and a kiss on his cheek and then watched as he climbed safely onto the loft.

The rest of the summer was spent finishing the schoolhouse construction and furnishing it with desks, blackboards and books. Li and Rose worked closely on the schoolhouse and spent quality time together, becoming closer every day. Li was cautious to not display his affection in public, knowing the harsh judgment that could arise from interracial relationships. Li and Cooper took daily horse rides together until Cooper was able to ride and care for Lhasa himself. Li found himself immersed in a world of love and contentment. He so enjoyed each day that he thought less and less about his other life, half a world away. When he did think about the Potala palace, it seemed like such a distant place, lost in time. It made him sad and confused, so he preferred to direct his thoughts more to the present and the happiness he found all around him.

On the first day of the new school year, Cooper was in charge of ringing the new school bell. From the front steps of the schoolhouse, he reached up and grabbed the rope tied to the bell and proceeded to jump up and down, as the bell rang far and wide for everyone to hear. After a few minutes, kids started to appear at the gate. Some were with their mothers and some were with their friends and siblings. Rose stood at the open gate and welcomed everyone back to school. There was excitement in the air, as the kids explored their new schoolhouse and playground. The moms all stood outside and gossiped with Rose until she excused herself and called the kids into the classroom. Li stood up by the barn, watching the kids arrive. He was proud of the work he had done on the schoolhouse and realized how important it was going to be to this community for years to come. When everyone had disappeared into class or back into town, Li grabbed his gloves and went to work building a new swing set and seesaw for the playground.

As everyone settled into the new school year, Li spent more time by himself and was able to resume his daily meditation routine. He preferred to rise before the sun so that he could enjoy the full natural beauty of a new day. One morning, Li was returning home from a walk down by the river. As he approached the bridge across the river, he saw Nathan approaching on horseback from the other direction. He was slouched deep into the saddle, half asleep, swaying back and forth to the slow rhythm of the horse's gait. He was obviously very tired and heavily intoxicated, no doubt returning home from another reckless night in the town saloon. Nathan had yet to see Li on the other side of the river, and Li thought about turning around and avoiding any confrontation. But as he looked across the bridge at Nathan, he could not help thinking of the horrific assaults he had thrust onto innocent women, and especially the woman he now loved so dearly. Then, in a split moment, he changed his mind. His heart began to race, and adrenaline filled his lifeblood, as he continued onto the bridge with a keen vigilance. As the horse entered the other side of the bridge, Nathan awoke and looked hazily across the bridge, not recognizing Li at first. The closer Li got to the horse, the greater his rage became. He had never felt such anger in his life, and everything suddenly went dark, as his mind blurred into the background.

"Hey, I know you," Nathan slurred as he lifted himself upright and pointed a limp finger at Li. "You owe me some money, you Chinese bastard."

Li remained silent and moved to the edge of the bridge as the horse began to walk past him.

Nathan pulled on the reins and stopped his horse next to Li. "Did you hear me, coolie? You stole my money!"

Li looked up at the disgraceful man swaying in his saddle. "I have no intention of returning any money to you."

"Yeah, well," Nathan said. "I'll just wait until you're gone and then go beat it out of that damn Rose."

It was then that rage took complete control over Li. He reached up and grabbed Nathan by his collar, yanked him from his horse, and slammed him violently onto the bridge. The horse jumped back and then bolted across the bridge, pushing Li to the ground as he passed. Li gathered himself and looked over at Nathan, who had lifted his bloodied head off the bridge and was attempting to sit up. Suddenly, his arms buckled, and his body went limp, as he collapsed over the edge of the bridge and rolled into the river.

Li stood up and walked across the bridge toward home. As he reached the end of the bridge, he glanced over his shoulder to see if Nathan had emerged from under the bridge. When Nathan did not surface, Li continued up the trail toward home, and then stopped. Standing above the riverbank, Li's mind cursed with conflicting thoughts. One moment he was convinced that karma had been served and he should just go home now. But then tightness in his chest grabbed hold and pulled his attention back toward the drowning man. Back and forth his thoughts ricocheted until he finally surrendered to the reality of his true self.

Li turned around and waded into flowing waters. Using the bridge as a handrail, he walked as far as he could and then submerged himself into the current and under the bridge. From under the bridge, he located the helpless body, dislodged it from the bridge and pulled it out of the water and onto the grassy bank. Sitting on the bank, he propped the man up from behind, wrapped his arms around the limp body and repeatedly thrust his fists into the chest, purging water from the lungs. Suddenly, the man gasped loudly and inhaled a breath of life. After a few rounds of coughing up water and taking in air, the man regained consciousness. Li rolled to one side and released Nathan onto the ground. He then stood up, looked one last time at the loathsome man, turned and walked away.

As the winter season moved in, the days got shorter and the nights got colder. Everybody had settled into a routine of managing school, chores, and playtime. Li and Cooper rode their horses together every chance they could. And Rose managed to teach school all day and still find time to cook supper most nights. It was more than the evenings that were challenging for Rose. She pulled back the covers and attempted to sit up in bed for the third time this morning and was, once again, consumed by queasiness and nauseous convulsions, forcing her back into bed. As she lay still in bed, she recognized the symptoms from her pregnancy with Cooper, years ago. She could not help but smile, thinking about telling Li and seeing his response to the news. Even though she was certain of her condition, she decided to visit the doctor in town before sharing the news with Li.

It was Saturday afternoon and Li was working in the barn when Rose walked in with a serious look on her face.

"Li," Rose said. "I have some news to tell you. Please come sit with me."

Rose and Li both sat on the hay bales inside the barn. Li could see the concern in Rose's eyes. As she sat down, her knees began to shake, and her hands clutched into a tight fist.

"What is it, Rose?"

"I don't know how else to say this," she said in a nervous voice. "I was in town earlier and everyone was talking about the president." Her eyes teared up. "Li, someone shot and killed President Lincoln!"

Li gasped out loud. "Oh, no," he said, overwhelmed by shock and disbelief. He was looking at Rose as the tears began to run down her cheek. He could see how upset she was. He reached over and put both his arms around Rose and pulled her close. She collapsed into his embrace and they both sat quietly in the barn, working through the emotions of such tragic news. Li continued to comfort Rose until she had stopped crying and stood up and faced Li.

"I know how much you liked President Lincoln and his wife," Rose said. "This must be very painful for you, and I want you to know how truly sorry I am that this happened."

"Thank you, Rose. It just does not seem real right now."

"That is understandable, Li," Rose replied. "Maybe after you get some rest."

Rose gathered herself, gave Li a soft kiss on his cheek, turned and walked up to the house.

Li went up to his loft and lay down on his bed. He was stunned by the news that President Lincoln was dead. His thoughts reflected on Mr. Lincoln and how kind he was to Li. His presence in the room never seemed overwhelming, and Li always felt that Mr. Lincoln listened patiently to him with genuine interest.

Li's mind drifted to the White House and what must be going on there. How was Mrs. Lincoln? That poor soul has been through so much death and suffering, she must be devastated. And the White House staff, how will they carry on with the pain of losing someone so close and so special?

Li wept quietly as he tried to process the impact this news must be having across the land. At some point, his thoughts drifted back home to the Potala palace. He wondered how Lhasa would handle such a tragic event. The idea seemed so remote, and yet he knew that there was political turmoil building in China that could escalate into Tibet. Suddenly, his sorrow turned to anxiety, fearing such an event could actually happen back home. He began to question his decision to leave the Potala palace. What are the High Lamas thinking right now about His Holiness? Was Panchen managing all right? Was Panchen willing to assume the role that was forced upon him by the Dalai Lama's departure? Was this all a selfish act on his part? Li found himself lost in a cyclone of inner thoughts. He sat up in his bed and tried and stop the chaos chasing through his mind.

Li drifted in and out of sleep all night, as he continued to work through his emotions. The following morning, he went for a long walk. He walked down to the river, where the water was flowing low and clear. He followed the river for a few miles, finally settling under a large cottonwood tree overlooking the winding waters. He sat on the ground, between two large roots, with his back resting against the broad trunk. The rippling sounds of the river calmed his mind, helping him to close his eyes and focus on his breathing. Slowly, Li drew in a deep breath, holding it for a few seconds before releasing it, along with his negative thoughts inside. Li repeated this cycle over and over. With each exhale, Li became more mindful of his inner thoughts, acknowledging each one before letting them dissolve into the background and allowing him to relax into natural awareness. From this lucid state, Li was able to explore the nature of his consciousness with perfect clarity. He confronted his doubts, his fears and his desires for the next several hours, eventually finding acceptance and forgiveness in his heart.

It had been months since Li was able to meditate on such a deep level. When he finally awakened, he felt a renewed sense of calmness and resolve. He stood up and returned to the Prairie Rose, with a full understanding of exactly what needed to be done.

CHAPTER TEN

Having just finished dinner, Cooper went up to his loft to read before bed. Li made a small fire in the fireplace while Rose finished cleaning in the kitchen.

"Would you like some coffee?" asked Rose.

"That would be nice, thank you."

Rose brought two cups of coffee over to the fire and handed one to Li before sitting down next to him on the sofa.

"I never imagined how much more effort it would take to teach eighteen kids versus ten kids last year," Rose said as she sighed heavily and rested her feet on top of the hearth.

Li smiled at Rose. "I admire your patience and enthusiasm."

They both sat quietly for a while, letting the evening fire soothe them into the night.

"Rose," Li said quietly. "I have something to tell you."

"I have something to tell you too, darling. But you go ahead first," Rose replied.

Li sat up straight and took a deep breath before speaking, "I think it is time for me to leave."

"Leave? And go where?"

"It is time for me to return to my homeland in Tibet."

Rose put her feet back on the floor and sat up facing Li. "But why? I thought everything was going so well."

"It is, Rose. Truly, it is. I have never been so happy in my life."

"Then why go back?"

"I have a responsibility back home and people who depend on me."

"You mean you have a family back there?"

"No," Li responded quickly. "Not a family, and not a wife." Li paused and thought carefully for a moment. "More like a congregation."

"You mean like a priest or something?"

"Yes, more like that."

"Oh, my goodness! Why didn't you say something before now?"

"I do not know, Rose. I guess I did not want to bring attention to that part of my life while I was in America."

"Well goddamn, Li. That's a pretty big deal to keep secret," Rose stated in some frustration as she stood up and went into the kitchen.

Li remained quiet, letting the emotions settle a bit.

"So, why are you telling me this now?" Rose asked. "Why is it suddenly so important that you return home?"

"I am not sure. I think when President Lincoln was

killed, I became fearful for my country and for the leaders over there."

"Are their lives in danger over there?" Rose asked.

"Not like here, certainly. But if anything did happen, I would feel horrible for not being there to help."

"So, just how large is your congregation?" she asked.

"I do not know, exactly. Several thousand, at least."

"Several thousand," Rose exclaimed in awe. "Are you a religious leader or a political leader?"

"Well, both, I suppose. You see, Buddhism has played a critical role in the development of Tibet throughout history. So, it is difficult to separate the spiritual influence from the political leadership."

Rose paused for a moment, to process this revelation. She looked closely at Li, trying to see if he looked any different to her. She had never seen him in this light and could not believe that he had been hiding such a large part of his life.

"So, why did you come here to America?"

Li felt somewhat confused. He had to think hard about how to answer this question.

"Well, to see the expansion and development of your country's frontier, and to learn about the impacts such development has on the native cultures and communities in its path."

"So, you always intended to go back someday," Rose concluded from his explanation.

"Perhaps, but I never imagined my experiences would

have such a personal impact."

"Oh, that's just great, Li," Rose snapped back. "You thought 'falling in love' would be just another observation to make note of in your journal."

Li and Rose sat quietly for a moment, diffusing the tension in the room.

"I'm going to bed," Rose stated. "Can you please put the fire out before you leave?"

"Of course, Rose," Li said as he stood to say good night.

Rose went up to her loft and dressed for bed. Her emotions were too elevated to fall asleep. As she lay in bed, she began to think back over the time she had known Li, trying to find a clue into his past. She recalled his strength and integrity, as he defended her from Nathan's attack. She remembered numerous times how generous he was— of both his time and his money. His enthusiasm and hard work were instrumental in the realization of the Prairie Rose School. His kindness toward everyone, especially her and Cooper, was nothing short of divine. The more she thought about Li, the more she understood who he was. He was such a simple man, and yet he made everyone around him feel exceptional. She realized that she had fallen in love with Li for the same reasons that all those people back in Tibet must love and rely on him. Rose realized that she could not ask Li to stay. As many reasons as she had for wanting him to stay, they were not as important as his world back in Tibet.

The following morning, Li came up to the house early

to fix coffee and breakfast.

The wonderful smell of freshly brewed coffee woke Rose up, and she grabbed her robe and proceeded down to the kitchen.

"Good morning, Li."

"Good morning, Rose," Li replied, handing her a hot cup of coffee.

"Li, I am sorry I got so upset last night," said Rose. "It was all such a surprise. I guess I became overwhelmed."

"Please, Rose, do not apologize. I realize that none of this makes any sense right now. And I am as confused as you are."

Li sat down at the table next to Rose.

"Rose, there is more to this story, that might help explain some things," Li started. "You see, I was raised in a very disciplined yet privileged world. Because of that, I felt like I had missed out on many of life's experiences. While I came to America for all of the reasons we discussed last night, I also came seeking knowledge about humanity and the nature of human existence." Li paused for a moment to gather his thoughts.

"Rose, please understand. I never expected that I would experience true love. And, even if I did, I could never have imagined how splendid and potent such love could be."

They both sat quietly at the table for a few minutes, letting their true feelings toward each other return.

"I thought a lot about this last night, Li," said Rose.

"Neither one of us could have predicted how our love came to be. I don't want you to leave. But I realize now, that is a selfish wish. For all of the joy and kindness you have brought to me and Cooper, I have no doubt that you have brought just as much to all those people back home. You see, these qualities are not restricted to your love for me or any one person. They are part of your soul, and you bring those qualities to everyone you meet. You have a gift, Li. And it needs to be shared with the world."

Li reached out and held Rose's hand tightly, as tears flowed from both of their hearts.

Li was in town to gather supplies for his trip but made a special stop at the lumber mill to see his friend James once more.

"I just wanted to say goodbye," Li said to James. "I am leaving soon to return to California, and then back home to Asia."

"Damn, Li. I am sorry to hear that," James replied. "It sure seemed like you were awful happy here in Omaha."

"I am happy here, as happy as I have ever been. But I have been away for a long time, and there are people back in my town who are expecting me to return."

"I understand," James replied politely. "I know there are a lot of folks here who are going to miss you, including me."

"Yes, and I will miss you, James," Li said.

"Which way are you planning to go out West?" James

asked.

"Well, I thought I would just follow the North Platte River, and then hook up with the California Trail."

"Yep, that's the best way," James said. "But you may run into winter trying to cross over South Pass. When you get to Fort Laramie, ask around and see how much snow is up on the pass. If there is still a lot of snow, you'll want to stay on the North Platte River until you can get through the mountains."

"Once again, your wisdom has come to my rescue," Li said as he extended his hand.

The two men shook hands firmly, and then James pulled Li closer and embraced him with a heartfelt hug. Li smiled at James as he turned and headed toward the door.

From the doorway, Li stopped and looked back at James. "James. I wonder if you might stop by and check on Rose once in a while. She has always been very fond of you, and I know she would enjoy your company. It would mean a lot to me too, knowing she was safe."

"I'd be happy to, Li. Don't you worry about a thing."

Li waved and smiled once more, before closing the door behind him.

Li was in the barn when school let out and Cooper wandered up to see what Li was doing.

"Is that a new horse, Li?"

"Yes, it is."

"Whoa, he's beautiful. What's his name?"

"This is Lucky," Li replied. "Lucky is going to be my partner all the way to California. I was just about to take him out for a ride. How would you like to ride along with me?"

"That would be great. I'll go tell Momma."

Li and Cooper rode down to the creek together, like they always did. Only this time it seemed different. Cooper was more quiet than usual. They both tied off their horses and sat down by the creek. Cooper picked up a handful of pebbles and began tossing them in the creek.

"Cooper, I know your Momma has told you about me leaving soon. Is there anything you would like to discuss with me?"

Cooper chose not to acknowledge the question immediately and continued tossing pebbles in the creek. Li sat quietly, knowing Cooper would speak when he was ready.

"Why do the people you love always leave?" Cooper finally responded.

"Well, it seems that way because it hurts so much more when you love the person who leaves. But just because someone has left, that does not mean they stop loving you, or that you should stop loving them."

"Well, it's mean, and it hurts, and I hate when it happens," Cooper asserted.

Li waited to respond, allowing Cooper to work through his emotions.

"When I was in school," Li reflected, "we were taught

that life is full of difficulties and suffering, such as sickness, old age, and eventually death to those you love most. And the suffering is greatest when you are attached to someone, so much that it distorts your thoughts and your actions."

Cooper had turned his back to Li, but he was clearly listening to what Li was saying.

"So, how do you stop the suffering?" Cooper asked.

"Well, like I said, suffering is part of life. But you can greatly reduce your suffering by focusing on those things that are in your control, such as your anger, your desires, and your fears."

"That sounds hard," Cooper replied.

Li thought for a moment. "Well, how about this? Just be kind, honest, and fair to all those around you."

"Kind, honest, and fair," Cooper repeated thoughtfully. "I can do that," he exclaimed with a broad smile.

"Then you will live a good life," Li replied, as he gave Cooper a big hug.

Li spent the next several days preparing for his departure. He finished up most of his projects around the Prairie Rose, including a beautiful stone path winding through Rose's garden. At the end of the path, Li had built a quiet sitting area under a small wood-framed pavilion, overlooking the vast prairie leading down to the river. In front of the bench seat was a small shrine made of stone and wood. The shrine was hand-built by Li and symbolized the one place in this world where he experienced pure Buddha nature.

One evening, while Li was sitting quietly in the pavilion, Rose walked up the path toward Li.

"My goodness, Li" Rose exclaimed as she approached Li. "The pavilion certainly turned out nice."

"Yes, well," Li replied. "It was mostly a selfish undertaking, as I hoped to use it for my mindfulness training. I guess that will not happen now."

Rose sensed the sadness in Li's voice. "Oh, my love. We are all a bit sad right now. But I am sure that sadness will fade with time, and the joy of our love and our time together will remain in our thoughts forever."

"Yes, that is how I wish to remember it as well," Li said with tears in his eyes.

"In fact, I feel something very special when I walk in here," Rose said as she looked around the pavilion. "I will come here often, to reflect on our love and pray for our grace and good fortune."

Rose sat down and snuggled close to Li and enjoyed the sunset with him one more time.

After packing his gear and stocking his saddlebags with the necessities to start his journey across the country, Li walked up to the house for supper. Cooper had just set the table and was sitting down to eat.

"You're just in time, Li," Rose said as she handed him a full plate.

"Thank you, Rose."

There was unease at the table, as everyone stared at their plates and ate quietly. It wasn't long before Cooper began to cry. He tried to hide his tears by wiping them away quickly and pretending no one noticed.

"It's all right, sweetheart," Rose said as she tried to console him. "We all feel the same way."

"I have a gift for you and your mom," Li said as he retrieved a bag from the desk by the doorway. "How would you like to open it?"

Cooper reached into the canvas bag and pulled out a beautiful wooden frame, with an oak stain and leather trim. Inside the frame was a handwritten poem.

"Momma, it is a poem written by Li," Cooper said.

"How nice," she replied. "Read it to us."

Cooper stood up and held the frame toward the lamp as he read.

THE JEWELS OF TIME

*The **Past** is gone. Learn and let go.*

*The **Future** is largely infinite and undetermined. Let hope be your compass.*

*The **Present** is Creation's gift to you. And what you think, say, and do in those precious moments reveals your true nature.*

- All my love, Li

"Oh, Li," Rose said softly. "That is so beautiful, it tears at my heart."

Rose reached out so Cooper could hand her the poem. She held it gently in her hands and read it to herself again. Then, she stood up and placed the gift at the center of the fireplace mantel, where it would be proudly displayed for all to see, forever.

The following morning, Li wanted to get an early start on his journey. He tried to be as quiet as possible while he prepared his coffee and bread in the kitchen, so as not to wake Rose and Cooper. Rose was already awake and came down soon after Li arrived. Li finished his breakfast then he and Rose walked outside to his horse.

"Saying 'goodbye' to you seems so final," Rose said.

"Perhaps. But we can always hope," Li said with a loving smile.

Li walked one final time through the gates of the Prairie Rose. He then turned and embraced Rose with a long and mournful hug.

"I love you, Rose," Li said as he held her close to his heart.

"I love you too, Li," Rose whispered behind her tears.

After another long embrace, Rose pulled away and let Li go. Li mounted his horse and smiled down at Rose one last time.

Just then, Cooper came out onto the porch in his sleepwear and hollered down to Li. "Goodbye, Li. I will never forget you."

Li waved back to Cooper with a big smile, and then he turned and rode towards the river. Rose walked back through the gate and up the stone path to Li's pavilion. From the pavilion, both she and Cooper watched as Li rode off into the distant prairie. As she watched him ride away, she cupped her hands gently around her new bulging belly, and with a contented smile on her face, she let her tears fall freely onto the ground.

CHAPTER ELEVEN

Li followed the creek down to the main river and proceeded along the worn trail next to the Platte River. After a few minutes on the trail, Li saw a man on horseback on the opposite side of the river. As he got closer, he recognized that it was Nathan on the horse. Li felt a sudden wave of nervous energy throughout his body, as he continued slowly up the trail. Nathan had stopped on the opposite riverbank, and his horse was taking a drink as Li rode by.

"Hey," said Nathan in a calm manner. "You're Li, right?"

"Yes," replied Li as he continued riding by slowly.

"Well, I just want you to know, you pulling me out of that river saved my life."

Li stopped and looked at the man across the river.

"I realize that now and just wanted to say, 'thank you,'" Nathan said.

Li let his guard down somewhat as his nerves settled.

Nathan sat up tall in his saddle and took off his hat,

"Truth is, I've done a lot of thinking these last few days. I am not proud of my behavior, and it is my intention to change my ways. It is also my intention to apologize to those that I have harmed, including Rose."

Li cringed when he heard her name coming out of that man's mouth. He wanted to believe Nathan, but his heart was not convinced.

"Well, I just wanted you to know before you left. I am gonna make things right," Nathan said with conviction.

With that, both men acknowledged a friendly gesture to each other and parted ways.

Riding along the Platte River trail was mostly level and quite easy. In fact, it became rather monotonous, causing the day to drag along slowly. Perhaps it was because Li was busy feeling sorry for himself. He could not stop thinking about all that he was leaving behind in Omaha. He had all that he could imagine ever wanting, and he was perfectly happy living at the Prairie Rose. The painful decision to leave Rose played over and over in his mind. He continued to have doubts about his decision to leave at all. His mind was confused and delusional as he wandered along the river. He told himself that this was a natural reaction to a natural emotion, and it would all pass eventually. As his mind continued to wander, he was no longer paying attention to the trail.

Suddenly, a large snake appeared lying on the trail ahead. Li did not see the snake in time to avoid it and was forced to step over it. With the snake slithering beneath Lucky, he reacted by leaping in the air and bolting off the trail. As he did, Li tried to hold on and gain control of Lucky but ended up sliding off the backside of his horse and onto the ground. As Li lay on the ground, he could not help but see the humor in the situation. He sat up and looked back to find Lucky standing just off the trail, waiting patiently. Li imagined how funny Cooper would have found this incident to be, and how he would probably still be laughing at Li. Li stood up and brushed himself off while laughing at himself under his breath. He then mounted Lucky and returned to the trail. From that point on, Li committed to maintaining a better focus on the path ahead and less on the path behind.

It took Li a few days to get accustomed to riding horseback from sunup to sundown. He eventually established a disciplined pace on the trail, while also allowing himself to enjoy the moments along the way. One afternoon, Li had set up an early camp along the river and was resting quietly on the riverbank watching the sunset. Every so often, he noticed a handful of birds would fly over in a V-shaped formation. These birds were extremely large with long legs, dusty white feathers, long craning necks, and wingspans that reached far from their bodies. Their heads were small and capped with brilliant red feathers, and a long narrow beak for probing the grasslands and shallow waters for food. The birds would communicate using a high-pitched bugle sound as they glided gracefully across the sky.

Once daylight began to wane, the birds started appearing in larger numbers. Li looked out at the distant sky and saw massive waves of birds flocking to the river. In a matter of minutes, there were tens of thousands of these huge birds converging onto the shallow riverbeds for a safe haven. The chorus of singing birds erupted into a tumultuous symphony that cheered on vigorously into the darkness of night. Once the birds had arrived safely on the sand bars of the Platte River, they slowly began to calm down and establish a comfortable roost for the night. What was once a mass of flapping wings and deafening noise that darkened the evening skies, quickly turned into a tapestry of quiet solitude spread harmoniously across the shallow river. Li sat quietly on the riverbank, trying not to disturb the natural perfection in front of him. He was in complete awe of the artistry and splendor of what was happening. After the cranes had all arrived and settled down for the night, Li stood up and walked back to camp in peaceful silence.

Li was fascinated by the contrasting nature he observed as he rode along the river. The river corridor was a green ribbon of life thriving on the precious water that meandered across the prairie. Large cottonwood trees, willows, wildflowers, and native grasses were all integrated along the banks of the river. This fertile ecosystem provided for a vast interdependent world of animal life, including insects, birds, rodents, snakes, fish, coyotes, foxes, antelope, deer, and buffalo. Meanwhile, just beyond the river corridor, lay the desolate dry plains that extended as far as the eye could see on both sides of the river. While not as elaborate as the verdant river corridor, the plains also hosted a different assortment of plants and animals that thrived perfectly well in the dry desert climate.

While riding through the prairie country, Li noticed something unusual in the distance. Instead of a flat plain covered in blond grasses and cacti, Li could see dark mounds spotted randomly far into the distant horizon. Li pulled off the river trail and moved toward the mounds on the plains. As he approached the open field, he was suddenly overcome by a foul stench permeating through the air. It was then he realized what he was seeing. The mounds were actually animal carcasses. His heart quickened as he covered his nose and mouth and tried to understand the cause of such devastation. The closer he got to the animals, the more he dreaded what he was seeing. He soon realized that the animals were buffalo, and they all had been scalped of their hides, leaving their naked remains rotting in the exposed desert sun. His racing heart quickly turned into a raging heart of fear, anger, and deep pain. Li dismounted his horse and began walking through the vast herd of dead carcasses spread across the prairie. He moaned quietly in anguish as he passed each corpse. He finally stopped in the middle of the heard, dropped to his knees and succumbed to the grief and sorrow he felt inside.

After praying for the lost lives of these precious animals, Li mounted his horse and rode slowly back to the river trail. As he rode back through the ruin, Li tried desperately to understand what would compel anyone to execute such an evil deed. His only conclusion centered around selfishness, greed, and a fundamental disconnect with the natural world. His anger continued as he rode until he finally became subdued by his heartfelt sorrow and grief.

After a long and arduous trip, Li finally rode into Fort Laramie just before sunset. Fort Laramie was a rather small town and served as a military outpost, trading post, Pony Express station, and a crossroads for several pioneer trails leading further west. Li unloaded his horse, secured a room in town, and immediately collapsed into his soft bed for a welcome nap. The nap turned into a full night's rest, and Li was awakened by the morning sun blazing through the window. Li rose from bed and proceeded outside to see what the town had to offer. He found the town to be quite unassuming with heavy military influence. However, despite the military presence, there seemed to be a wide diversity of people and interests in such a small concentration. There were tipi camps outside of town, where native Indians resided while trading their handmade crafts for food, clothing, and liquor. Several emigrant wagons had also set camp at the edge of town while they replenished their supplies and waited patiently for the snow to melt in the high country. In town, there were several military buildings, as well as few small cafés, saloons, and general store under private ownership. Li sought out a place serving breakfast and proceeded inside.

Following breakfast, Li went to the general store to replenish supplies and to get information on the condition of the South Pass.

"Good morning, sir," said the man behind the counter. "What can I do for you?"

"Good morning," Li replied. "I need some food supplies to get me over the mountains."

"Absolutely. Right over here," he said walking and pointing to the back wall. "We got dried fruit, jerky, coffee, sugar, oatmeal, and hard biscuits. Help yourself."

"Thank you, sir." Li grabbed a couple of burlap sacks and began to fill them with an assortment of supplies. He then grabbed another canteen and a box of matches on his way back to the counter.

"Where you headed?" asked the store clerk.

"San Francisco."

"Oh yeah. Lots of people heading out that way these days."

"What can you tell me about the snow on South Pass right now?" Li asked.

"Well, it's still not passable," said the man. "Probably another week or two, I'd say."

"I see," Li said as he paid for his supplies and gathered

the sacks to leave.

"If you didn't want to wait," the man said. "You could follow the river further south into Colorado Territory. From there, you can head west and cross over the mountains."

"All right. How much farther south?"

"Oh, in about five or six days you're gonna reach the river's headwaters in a large open valley. From there, you'll see a low spot in the mountains to the west. Cross through that saddle and head west until you meet the ocean."

"I'm sure it is not as easy as you make it sound," Li replied. "But I can do that."

"Well, I'm not gonna lie to you, son. It's gonna be a long and rugged ride to California."

"Well, thank you for the information and for the supplies," Li said as he turned to exit the store.

On his way out of the general store, another man walked in. The man was small in stature, with long dirty hair and beard surrounding his dark wrinkled face. He was dressed in ragged clothing, with a stale odor that permeated the store upon his arrival.

"*Hello, monsieur,*" said the man in a strong French accent. "*Can I interest you in some premium buffalo skins,*" he said as held out a handful of hides that still had blood dripping from them.

"No, absolutely not," The store clerk hollered out. "I already have a stack of those in back that I can't sell. Get those smelly pelts out of my store."

The Frenchman stopped for a moment to prepare his next sales pitch. Before he could say another word, the store clerk had come around from the counter and was waving the man out before the stench overwhelmed his store.

"Out!" yelled the clerk. "Take all of that shit outside."

The man had no choice but to turn around and exit the store while throwing expletives in French back to the store clerk.

Li watched the whole exchange from inside the store. When the encounter was over, Li smiled as he walked by the clerk holding the door open, trying to clear the foul smell out of his store.

"Well, sir," Li said to the Frenchman standing in the street. "At least you will make good money from the delicious meat that you harvested from your buffalo."

"*Oh, I think not, monsieur. I left the meat on the animal in the field. It was much too difficult to preserve and transport into town.*"

"I see," Li said somewhat sarcastically. "Perhaps you should leave the hunting to the local Indians. They have been successful at harvesting the buffalo in this country for generations."

The Frenchman threw another hand gesture in the air, as he walked away spouting expletives to whoever would listen. Li shook his head in disgrace as he waved once more to the store clerk.

Li walked casually through town and ended up at the Indian trader's tables set up near the tipi camp. He bought a beautiful Indian blanket from one of the families, figuring it would be for a good cause as well as for good use. It did not take long for Li to see all that the small town had to offer. He decided to have an early supper and prepare his gear for an early departure in the morning.

As soon as Li left the town of Fort Laramie, he noticed significantly fewer people following the trail into Colorado Territory. Though not a major concern, he could not help but wonder if he should have waited for the South Pass to open, like the rest of the west-bound emigrants. Those thoughts were short-lived, and Li soon found comfort in the quiet solitude on the trail. He was well rested, well supplied, and well prepared for whatever was to come his way.

After following the river through a narrow, winding canyon, Li emerged onto a broad valley at the river's headwaters. The valley sat at a high elevation, surrounded by spectacular Rocky Mountains in every direction. The valley floor was covered in montane grasslands, and sweet-smelling sagebrush filled the thin air and cool breeze. Looking out across the broad wind-swept basin reminded Li of his homeland and he became homesick for the first time since he arrived in America. He thought about the towering peaks behind the Potala palace, and how he and Lobsang loved riding out onto the grasslands to watch the nomads tending to their livestock. Or how the morning frost adhered so tightly to the bare tree branches, they looked like trees made from crystals. Longing for his home again only reaffirmed his decision to leave America. However, as he reflected on his memories of home, he felt somewhat detached from his thoughts and saw his visions more from an outsider looking in, than as a memory from his personal past. He realized just how long he had been away and imagined the changes that had occurred these past few years since he left his homeland.

From atop an elevated outcrop in the valley, Li easily identified the low saddle crossing through the mountains on the west side. The rest of the day was spent crossing the broad valley. Li reached the forested hillside at the foot of the mountain pass just before sunset. He rode into the forest for a while and then looked for a place to set camp for the night. As he approached a small opening in the trees, he noticed smoke rising above the tree line. Li dismounted from Lucky and walked silently toward the smoke. When he reached the edge of the opening, he could see the fire coming from a camp in a small meadow. Li stood hidden in the trees to survey the camp before he made any contact. The campfire was blazing high into the sky, illuminating the entire meadow. A man was sitting beside the fire with a blanket draped over his shoulders. The man had long dark hair, tied into two long braids with simple beads and a feather tied to each end. From the looks of the man and his blanket, Li concluded that he must be a native Indian. And with only one horse tied to a tree nearby, he also appeared to be alone. Li continued to watch the man from afar. The man was sitting cross-legged, facing the fire, and remained very still, as if he might be meditating. After a few minutes of sitting quietly, the Indian began to recite some sort of chant. He first started by humming in a low rhythmic sound. He would hold a single note for what seemed like an eternity, and then change his pitch slightly and hold that note for another extended period. The rhythm of his mantra slowly increased, and the man began swaying his body to the rhythm as he transitioned from one extended note to another. Eventually, the energy in the Indian's body was more than he could contain. He stood up and began walking around the blazing fire, all the while chanting and swaying rhythmically. The man's walk quickened into a skip, as his voice raised to a full crescendo. At its peak, the Indian hopped and skipped wildly as he chanted and wailed at the night sky. Li secretly watched the man for several minutes. He concluded that the Indian must be performing some sort of ritual. Not wanting to disturb the ceremony, Li decided it might be best if he stayed away from the camp until morning. He slowly backed away from the camp before mounting his horse and riding deeper into the forest to find another campsite for the night.

The following morning, Li woke up early and made a small campfire to take the chill off and to heat his morning coffee. After breakfast, Li broke camp and rode back over to the Indian's camp. He once again dismounted and quietly approached the camp from behind the trees. The Indian was up and cooking breakfast over a small fire. Li tied Lucky to a nearby tree and walked into camp barehanded.

"Good morning, sir," Li said from the camp perimeter.

The Indian rose quickly to his feet and faced Li. He then quickly scanned in every direction, nervously looking for more strangers in the trees.

"I am alone, and I mean no harm," Li pleaded, with his hands in the air.

"Who are you? Where did you come from?" The Indian demanded in simple broken English.

"My name is Li. I am alone and traveling west over the mountains."

The Indian looked around again, surprised that someone had found him. "Where did you come from?" the Indian asked again.

"I have been riding for several days. I camped at the bottom of the hill last night. I am alone and mean no harm to you. Do you understand?"

The Indian relaxed somewhat but remained nervous and cautious. He was obviously surprised by Li's appearance, "Yes, I understand," he finally replied.

Li looked closer at the Indian. He was very young, maybe seventeen or eighteen years old. He was dressed in worn leather leggings and a buckskin shirt decorated with colored dyes and beads. He was a fairly short man but stood tall, very lean and strong. His eyes were dark and narrow but had a shade of youthful innocence in them as well.

"May I sit down?" Li asked.

"Yes," replied the Indian. They both sat down on some boulders near the fire. "How did you find me?"

"I saw the smoke from your fire."

The Indian had calmed down a little, but his nervousness seemed to turn into some sort of sorrow.

"What is your name?"

"My name is Ouray."

"My name is Li. I am pleased to meet you."

"You must go," the Indian said.

"Is everything all right?"

"Yes, but I am on a journey and I must travel alone."

"I understand," Li replied. "I do not intend to travel with you. May I rest by your fire for a moment?"

"Yes, of course," said Ouray, trying to control his nervousness.

"You speak good English," Li said, trying to break the silence. "Where did you learn?"

"In the Southern Basin," Ouray said. "There are many outposts with English speaking people there. Also, many Spanish people. I speak some Spanish too."

The two men sat quietly by the fire. As Li surveyed the camp, he could tell that Ouray had been there for a while. There was a rope tied between two trees, with horse blankets draped over it. There was also a large stack of firewood in the trees. Next to the fire, there was a cairn of rocks stacked on one side, and a circle of rocks about six feet in diameter laid down neatly on the other side.

"Where are you going on your journey?" Li asked.

"Well, it is not so much a journey. I have been sent here by my tribe as a rite of passage into manhood. It is called a *vision quest*."

"Oh. And you must make this quest alone?"

"Yes. I am afraid if my elders see you here, it will be a very bad sign for my future."

"I understand."

"They are not nearby now. I was frightened when you came into camp. I am sorry," Ouray said softly under his breath.

"Do not apologize. How far away is your home?"

"We have a summer camp in the Yampa Valley, about four days from here. We spend winters in the Southern Basin."

"And how did you find this site for your *vision quest*?"

"This is one of the Ute spirit sites used by my tribe. It is located near the 'Rabbit Ears,' where the gods can hear our prayers and give us guidance." Ouray stood up and pointed to a pair of rock outcrops at the top of the hill. "There, those are the Rabbit Ears," he said.

"Yes, I can see that." said Li.

After things had settled down, Ouray became more engaging.

"Where are you going?" asked Ouray.

"California."

"Is that where you live?"

"No, I live across the ocean. California is where I will get on a ship to return home."

"Where have you been?"

"Well, I started in California working on the railroad. And I eventually found my way to Washington, DC, where I worked for President Lincoln."

"You worked for the president?" Ouray said with newfound excitement.

"Yes. Did you know him too?"

"I know him, but not personally. My tribe is worried about the white man coming into our territory. And many of my elders think it is because of President Lincoln."

"Yes, well, the white man is coming," Li said with certainty. "But I do not believe President Lincoln is the one to blame."

Suddenly, Ouray sat up straight and looked directly at Li with a serious, almost shocked expression. His eyes scanned up and down the man sitting on the rock next to him.

"Are you all right, Ouray?" asked Li, noticing his wide eyes and suddenly pale face. "Did I say something wrong?"

Ouray stood up quickly and walked around the camp with his hands on his head in disbelief. He began talking to himself in his native tongue as he paced back and forth. From the other side of the fire, Ouray suddenly stopped and looked over at Li. He then walked back to where Li was sitting. He reached out and touched Li on his shoulder. Then he reached out with his other hand and embraced Li's other shoulder. While still in a confused state, Ouray released his hands from Li and sat back down on the rock.

"What is it, Ouray?"

"I am not sure," Ouray replied. "But I had a vision last night that a guardian spirit was coming."

"What is a guardian spirit?"

"They can be anything, but mostly they are sacred messengers and symbols of divine power."

"Well, as you can see, Ouray, I am a man just like you," Li stated purposefully. "I may come from a land far away, and I may have seen things that could be helpful to you and your people. But I believe divine power is available to each of us, only after we have cleared the path."

Ouray smiled back at Li. "You sound like my grandfather. *'The river of truth is always clear,'* he would say. *'It is our mind that muddies the waters.'*"

"Your grandfather sounds like a wise man."

Ouray became noticeably more relaxed around Li. He prepared a cup of hot tea and a plate of food for each of them and then sat down to learn more about Li's experiences with the white man.

"It may be true that President Lincoln helped to build the railroad across America," Li expanded on the conversation. "But he saw this as progress, and a resource for improving people's lives."

"But, if the railroad brings the white man into Indian territory, how will that improve the Indian's life?"

"Well, there is much good to be learned from the white man. But I must warn you, they are filled with self-determination, and they will stop at nothing if they feel they are entitled."

The longer Ouray listened to Li, the more convinced he was that Li had some kind of spiritual awareness and possessed knowledge that could help the Ute tribe. He felt sure that his dreams had been answered, and he must take full advantage of the vision he had been given.

"Li, I have been sent to these mountains by my elders to seek answers and guidance, so that I may return home and lead my people into the future," Ouray said. "I came here not knowing what that meant, or how I would recognize that when I saw it. But now, I feel like you are that answer. You have a vision into the future that could be of great benefit to the Ute tribe. I know I told you that I must complete this quest on my own. But this is so important to my people, I do not want to fail. If you would just come back with me, I am sure I can convince my elders to listen to you."

Li thought carefully about the proposal. "I am happy to share what I have seen during my time in America," Li said. "We can ride together for a while and discuss all of this in greater detail. If you still feel strongly about this when we get to your village, I will meet with your elders."

The two men proceeded to break camp and begin their

journey west to the Ute summer camp in the Yampa Valley. While the two men rode alongside the river, they engaged in endless discourse about topics close to their familial hearts. They found common ground in much of their past, present and future situations. Ouray listened especially intently to Li's observation of the white man and their imminent expansion across the frontier.

"They call it *Manifest Destiny*," Li said. "It is not a policy or a government plan. It is more like a sacred duty or an unbridled conviction to expand across the American territories under the providence of God. While it sounds like a virtuous cause, it has become an entitlement to many people, leading to discrimination, greed, and violence on the frontier."

"Yes, but if the land is part of our ancestral land, doesn't that mean they are trespassing," Ouray asked.

"Apparently not. They see all of the western frontier as free land. In fact, the government is giving ownership to anyone who settles a plot of land and uses it for domestic farming or ranching."

"My people are hunters, not farmers. We have hunted these lands for centuries. We go where the animals go. To the deserts in the winter and the mountains in the summer."

"I understand, Ouray. I just do not think the white man will care."

Ouray became visibly distraught from the conversation with Li and began to ride slowly and quietly behind Li for a while, where he remained for the rest of the day. It saddened Li to see his friend so despondent. He continued to ride alone most of the afternoon, periodically looking back to see where Ouray was. With sunset coming, Li found a place to rest for the night. He dismounted Lucky and began setting up camp. There was plenty of deadwood beneath the large cottonwood trees that lined the river. Li built a fire ring on the grass beneath the cottonwoods and stacked the firewood nearby. He was unloading his saddlebags when Ouray arrived in camp.

"Just in time, Ouray. I was about to start supper," Li said holding out a can of beans and a bag of hard biscuits.

"No, my friend," Ouray said with a big smile. "Tonight, we eat fish for dinner." Ouray dismounted his horse, tied him off to a tree, and pulled a small leather sack out of his saddlebag.

"Fish for dinner?" Li replied in a skeptical tone.

"Oh, yes. Fishing is a skill learned by Ute boys at an early age."

Ouray proceeded to remove a long piece of braided hemp that gradually became thinner and thinner until it was almost invisible. Ouray then removed a small section of bone from the sack, that had been filed and polished into the shape of a hook with a very sharp tip at one end. Ouray looked around on the ground until he found a long willow branch. He tied the thick end of the braided line to one end of the willow branch and the thin end of the line to the bone hook.

"Now we just need something good for the fish to eat," Ouray said, as he removed a bone handle hunting knife from his bag. He then walked along the riverbank looking for something to attach to his hook. Before long, Ouray returned to camp with an assortment of options to entice the trout. He stuck the bone hook through a grasshopper, gave Li a big smile and proceeded down to the river. From behind a willow bush, Ouray stopped and studied the water surface features closely. He then lowered to his knees and crawled to the bank. Li followed Ouray to the water on his knees, to watch the action. From a kneeling position, Ouray held the willow branch up over the water as high as he could, and then with a flip of his wrist launched the grasshopper upstream and into a slow drifting ripple near the bank. Li watched the grasshopper hit the water and begin drifting in the current back toward Ouray. Suddenly, the water roiled around the hopper. Ouray quickly lifted the willow branch into the air, securing the hook into the fish's mouth.

"Got it!" Ouray said loudly as he stood up near the bank. There was a violent splash in the water, and then a large trout leaped out of the river in a spectacular display of force, before crashing back down into the water. Ouray walked briskly down the river, keeping a firm tension on the line to the fighting trout. Li followed the battle downstream in complete astonishment. At one point, Ouray was forced into the river to keep up with his adversary. In water up to his waist, Ouray held on tight to the valiant warrior until the trout eventually tired and surrendered. When the fish had completely surrendered, Ouray led the fish to the bank and reached into the shallow water and lifted the beautiful trout out of the river, onto the grassy bank. After removing the hook from the mouth of the trout, Ouray held the fish into the air and gave thanks to the higher powers that brought him this meal.

"Oh my," exclaimed Li with joy and excitement. "That was simply amazing!"

"I'm glad you enjoyed that. Now it is your turn."

"What?"

"Yeah, I got my dinner. Now you must catch yours."

"You are not serious," Li said.

"Yes, I am serious. Unless, of course, you do not want fish for dinner."

Li was sure that Ouray was kidding, but he was quite intrigued by what he had just witnessed.

"Okay, I will try. But you must help me learn how."

Ouray caught another grasshopper in the grass and handed it to Li. "Now push the hook in the head of the grasshopper and back again through the tail."

Li took the grasshopper in one hand and the hook in the other. He stood there for some time looking at the challenge before him, obviously conflicted by his emotions.

"I am sorry, Ouray," Li said in a serious tone. "I cannot willingly kill the grasshopper or the fish. It is against my religious principles to intentionally kill living things."

"Are you sure?" said Ouray. "My people believe in the rightful existence of all living things as well. That is why we take only what we need and give thanks for every sacrifice made on our behalf."

"Yes, and I would be most thankful for such a sacrifice as well," Li stated. "Perhaps I can find it in my heart to accept the meal caught and prepared by a true native of these lands."

"That sounds fair," Ouray said as he took the grasshopper from Li. "You go start the fire, and I will catch you a fish for dinner."

"That sounds good," Li replied as he handed the willow branch and hemp line back to Ouray. "I enjoyed watching you more anyway."

The fire had just been lit when Ouray walked into camp with two beautiful fish in hand. Li could only shake his head and bow to the master fisherman before him.

When the fish had been cooked to perfection, Ouray handed one of the fish skewers to Li and then held the other in both his hands. "I speak to the creator in our heavens and give thanks for providing us with this meal tonight. We understand the sacrifices made for our benefit and are most grateful."

Ouray then looked over at Li. "Would you like to add anything, Li?"

Li looked down at the fish in his hands. After some reflective personal thought, his mind aligned with his heart, and Li replied, "No, I am fine. Thank you."

"Well, then let's eat," said Ouray.

On the last morning before the men were scheduled to arrive at the Ute village, they broke camp early and rode along the trail together and discussed in greater detail how Ouray would introduce Li to his father and the Council of the Elders and what exactly they intended to say to the council.

"I have told you enough about the white man for you to explain the dangers facing the Ute tribes," Li said. "I think it would be best for you to lead the conversation and I will support you with details if necessary."

"Yes, I agree," Ouray stated. "They will be reluctant to trust you, so it would be best for me to do most of the talking."

"I am confident that you know what risks your people are facing. It is important that you state those risks clearly to your elders and focus their attention on finding solutions so that they do not become fearful and angry. That will only lead to poor thinking and irrational decisions."

"Yes, I agree," Ouray said. "Thank you, Li, for giving me the confidence to face my people as a leader. It is important to me and my father that I follow the family tradition and become a respected chief in the Ute tribe."

"I have no doubt that you will be a great and compassionate chief."

As the men reached the ridgetop overlooking the small

valley where the Ute camp resided, Ouray suddenly stopped and stood up in the stirrups on his horse. He looked intently down into his village, trying to piece together what he was seeing.

"What is it, Ouray?"

"I don't know, but there are problems in camp," Ouray said as he sat back in the saddle and sprinted down the hill toward his encampment. Li followed closely behind Ouray, not knowing exactly what to expect in the village.

The closer they got to the encampment, Li could see smoke rising from the village, several tents had been torn to the ground and set afire, and numerous horses were standing untied around the camp. When they reached the center of camp, Ouray dismounted and quickly ran into his father's tent.

"Father, what has happened?" Ouray said in his native language.

His father was sitting cross-legged on the ground next to his mother, and they were both facing Ouray's grandfather, who was lying motionless on the ground before them.

"Oh, Ouray," his mother exclaimed as she stood up and embraced him. "I am so glad to see you."

"Are you all right, Mother?"

"Yes, dear. Are you?" she asked.

"Yes, I am fine," replied Ouray as he embraced his mother while looking over her shoulder at his father sitting quietly on the ground next to Papa.

Ouray kissed his mother's cheek and then knelt down next to his father, who was clearly in a painful state of grief. Chief Murah was a stoic man of few words. He carried the burden of over one hundred Utes in his tribe along with a seat at the council representing all Ute bands throughout the west. Ouray had never seen his father cry before. He put his arm gently around his father and held him close, and they both wept quietly over Papa.

Outside the chief's tent, Li found several residents working diligently to clean up the damage to their village. He immediately engaged in assisting the effort in whatever way he could. He helped clean up the village for the remainder of the afternoon, while Ouray stayed in the tent alongside his family in mourning. When the sun had set, and it was too dark to continue, Li excused himself and retreated into the forest outside of the village, where he made camp for the evening.

The following morning, Li made himself some coffee and biscuits for breakfast and then rode back into the encampment to assist with the relief effort. As he entered the camp, he saw Ouray outside helping with the cleanup.

"Good morning Ouray. Is your family safe?" asked Li.

"Yes, I think everything is fine now. However, my grandfather has been killed."

"Oh, I am so sorry, Ouray. I cannot imagine the grief in your family."

"Thank you. Unfortunately, several tribal families are grieving over their losses as well."

"Yes, I suspected that from what I saw yesterday. What do you know about the incident?"

"They were ambushed in the early morning," Ouray stated. "Most people think it was a cavalry outpost from Salt Lake City. They have been patrolling the western territories for some time."

While the two men were talking outside, Ouray's father walked by them on his way back to his tent. Ouray started to say something but immediately sensed anger and disapproval in his father as he walked by with a stern look on his face and entered the tent without acknowledging his son.

"That was my father," Ouray said. "I better go."

Li watched Ouray enter the Chief's tent and then returned to assist the villagers with the cleanup effort.

Inside the Chief's tent, Chief Murah was preparing Papa's body for the funeral ceremony. "Who is that stranger you were speaking to?"

"His name is Li. I met him on the trail near Rabbit Ears. He is a traveler from across the ocean. He has been to Washington, DC, and has met the president."

"Why is he here?"

"Father, he came into my camp after my fire dance. He is most knowledgeable about the white man."

"So, you think he is some sort of spirit god," Chief replied with skepticism.

"I do not know. But he told me this would happen," Ouray stated as he pointed outside the tent. "And there is more danger coming."

"We will not speak of this now," Chief Murah stated in a distracted and frustrated voice. "We have a lot of work to do, and I will not address this situation until after the funeral ceremony."

It was Ute tradition for the deceased to remain inside the family lodge with the family until the day of the funeral. This allowed time to grieve in privacy while preparing the body and personal belongings. Because there were numerous deaths on this occasion, almost every family in the tribe was impacted. That left very few people available to construct the platforms for the cremation ceremony. As soon as Li understood what needed to be done, he engaged fully and became a very useful resource. He immediately began collecting logs and branches from the nearby forest, piling them into an open field that had been designated as the cremation site. The available Ute men constructed enough wooden beds to hold all of the deceased. As soon as the beds were completed Li helped stack several bundles of smaller branches underneath the platforms.

By sunset, the pyres had all been completed and were ready for the ceremony. The families of the deceased had cleaned the bodies and wrapped them in hides along with personal belongings and spiritual objects from the family. When darkness had fallen, the entire tribe stood side by side, forming a procession line from the funeral pyres to the first tipi. The family members carried their deceased out of the tipi and through the tribal procession to the ceremonial platforms. The procession line moved to every tipi one at a time, until all of the deceased had been delivered to the funeral ceremony. As the tribal members gathered around the pyres, a medicine man performed a number of rituals to bless the spirits of the deceased and to pray for a safe passage into the afterlife. Then, as a few men lit a fire beneath the platforms, the tribal members all chanted together and sang traditional songs handed down from their ancestors. Li was moved to tears by the ceremony. He stood in the shadows of darkness and silently wept for the deceased and for his friend's suffering.

The following morning, Li was resting at his camp on the outskirts of the village when Ouray arrived.

"Good morning, Li."

"Good morning, Ouray. How are you today?"

"I am better, thank you. My village is still very upset, but I believe the ceremony last night was helpful."

"Yes, I was quite moved by the event as well."

"Li, my father has asked if you would attend a meeting with the elders this afternoon. I have explained as much as I know about you and have told them that your experiences may be useful to us in our future with the white man."

"Of course, Ouray. I would be honored."

"I must warn you; my father is a very strong-headed man. He will listen carefully to what you say, but he rarely changes his mind. I suggest you tell the elders what you have told me about the white man, and then let them discuss what should be done."

"I understand," Li replied. "I hope you will be part of the discussion as well. This is your vision, and it is your future. You need to be part of the solution."

"Perhaps, but the Council of Elders are very traditional. I am still new to the council and hardly ever provide guidance. But I will do my best."

"But Ouray, it is your guidance that is most important, because it is you and the young members of your tribe that must live with the consequences of the actions taken today. Our elders can teach us a lot, but we must also recognize and accept our role in building our future."

Li paused and reflected on what he just said. Those words were meant for Ouray, but they resonated deeply within himself. For the first time, Li realized the significance of holding the future of so many souls in the actions he chose to take every day.

The two men sat quietly, basking in the morning sun, both thinking about a similar future, but in two completely different worlds.

Li followed Ouray into the elder's lodge, where all of the council members had been gathered for most of the day. The elders stood and warmly greeted their new guest. Li was escorted around to shake hands with each elder and then was presented with a traditional ornament of woven leather, beads, and feathers. Li gratefully accepted the gift and then sat down next to Ouray.

Chief Murah spoke in his native language, while Ouray translated for Li.

"I have been told by the elders that you have been most helpful to my village over the past couple of days. We are all grateful for your help and support."

The elders all bowed gently to Li.

Li then bowed in return. "Thank you, Chief. My heart goes out to the families suffering from their losses."

"We meet as a council today to discuss the tragedy that has been thrust onto our community, and to determine our response to this action. Ouray has told us that the completion of the railroad will only bring more white men into our lands, causing even greater tragedies and losses. He says you are the one who has told him these stories?"

"What Ouray has told you is true, sir," Li responded. "The railroad will be capable of transporting thousands of people into the west every day. Today, it may take months to cross the country. Tomorrow, it will be done in only a few days."

"It is the position of the elders that we must react quickly and forcefully to this threat before it reaches such a large scale."

"I understand your position, Chief," Li said. "But the white man will not retreat. They see their people as naturally superior to all other people. This self-proclaimed status has already caused great pain and suffering to the Black man, and it will do the same to the native Indian."

"Father, Li is right. He has witnessed the white man at war with themselves. They have killed hundreds of thousands of their own people in the Civil War. They will certainly not care who dies out here."

Li suddenly felt the air leave the room. The harsh reality of what they had just heard overwhelmed the elders. He noticed a more concerned look on their faces, including Chief Murah's.

"Then how are we to live alongside such a savage culture?" asked the Chief.

"Not all white men are savages, Chief," Li stated. "In fact, they have many of the same qualities as the Ute tribe. They have strong family values. They are kind and compassionate to those in their community. And they have a core spiritual belief, which provides them with great joy and happiness. Their anger originates from fear, just like yours or mine. That is why it is best to approach this situation without threats of violence." Li looked over at Ouray for translation.

Ouray translated to the elders and then felt empowered by Li to respond. "If I may speak to the council," Ouray addressed the Chief. "I agree that we must act quickly to avoid further losses and pain to our people. But we cannot win this war on the battlefield. If we bring two hundred warriors to battle, they will bring 2,000. If we bring 2,000, they will bring 20,000."

Ouray paused to see if he still had everyone's attention. "The best hope for our people is to negotiate an agreement that recognizes our natural rights to continue living where we are, as who we are, for as long as we are here."

"The white man does not seem interested in negotiations with the native Indians," Chief Murah stated.

"The white men on the frontier are not the ones to negotiate with," Li replied. "You must arrange a meeting with the current president and his people. They are the only ones who can make an agreement."

"Why would the President of the United States be interested in meeting with a small Ute band in the mountains?" the Chief asked.

"He may not," said Li. "But more than anything, the president wants peace in America. If you organized all of the Ute bands together and even included other native Indian tribes, then he will find interest in what you propose. The larger the coalition, the more leverage you will have."

The elders all sat quietly staring at each other. Such a proposal had never been made in front of the council before.

"I will discuss this further with the council and we will decide what is best for our tribe," the Chief said as he stood to escort Li outside. Li stood up and bowed to the Council of Elders, and then walked out with Ouray and the Chief.

The Chief shook hands with Li and thanked him for his advice to the council. He then turned to address his son. *"Ouray, I would like you to sit with me in the council while we discuss this further."* Ouray watched his father walk into the lodge and then turned to follow him in. He quickly looked back at Li with a broad smile before disappearing into the lodge.

Li returned to his camp and began to prepare for his departure. He was sitting by the fire after supper when Ouray rode into his camp.

"Hello, Li. May I join you?"

"Of course, Ouray. Please sit. I have some beans left if you are hungry."

"No, thank you. I have had supper," Ouray replied as he sat down by the fire.

"How are the grieving families this evening?" asked Li.

"Better. I think the funeral ceremony allowed for the acceptance of our losses and helped release us from our suffering."

"I hope you are right," said Li.

"So, I think we made some good progress with the Council of Elders," said Ouray.

"Oh, that is wonderful. I could see they were surprised, and perhaps confused, by the information that we shared with them."

"Yes, they most certainly were," Ouray said smiling. "And no one more so than my father."

"Well, he carries a heavy burden on his shoulders. It may take more than words to change his mind."

"He has decided to present the proposal to all of the Ute bands when we assemble at the annual Bear Dance."

"That is a great idea."

"Actually, he has asked me to present the proposal to all of the Ute bands," Ouray stated proudly.

"Hey, that's even a better idea," Li replied. "I must say, you really handled yourself well in the lodge today, Ouray."

"Thank you, Li. I felt so empowered with you sitting next to me. You gave me great confidence."

"You are ready to do great things, Ouray. And you have given me the guidance I need to meet my future as well."

The two men sat peacefully next to the fire. They spoke periodically. But mostly they sat quietly, letting the natural realities of life absorb them.

The following morning, Li packed his bags and rode into the Ute camp one last time. He found Ouray sitting with his father outside their tents. Li dismounted his horse and joined Ouray.

"So, you are heading west today?" asked Ouray.

"Yes."

"Well, stay on the north side of the river."

"Okay, thanks."

"And, once the river turns to the south, I suggest following it for at least a few more days. If you cut to the west too soon, you will find nothing but hot, dry desert."

"Oh, that sounds like good advice."

Li then turned to the chief. "Chief Murah. I want to thank you for your kindness and generosity toward me. I feel blessed to have met you and your wonderful people. This has been an experience I will not forget."

Chief Murah stood up and approached Li. With his hands on Li's shoulders, he said a few short words in his native tongue before embracing Li with a firm hug.

Li looked over at Ouray. "He said he admires you. You are a man of great strength and great kindness," Ouray translated.

"Thank you, sir," said Li as he bowed in reverence to the chief.

As Li began to leave, one of the elders approached him. He was the medicine man from the village. He handed Li a string of beads and then said to Li, "*I have seen your soul, my son. It sits at the right hand of the spirit god. You have been given the highest blessings to safely cross our native heartland.*" He then turned and walked away.

Ouray walked with Li to the edge of the village. They were both quiet, as words could no longer capture their feelings. There were tears in the eyes of both men, as they faced and hugged goodbye. Li mounted his horse, smiled down at his friend once more and then rode away.

CHAPTER TWELVE

Leaving the Ute village, Li felt a renewed energy. Using the river as his guide, Lucky was able to follow along without much guidance from Li. This allowed Li to let his thoughts wander aimlessly from topic to topic. He reflected on how much he had learned on his journey to America and how anxious he was to share it with the High Lamas back in Lhasa. He thought about Lobsang, and how much he would have enjoyed traveling together with Li. He thought about how long it had been since he had been home and wondered what had changed since he left.

After several days of following the river, Li began to drift westward toward California. The river had disappeared into a deep canyon and was no longer in sight. The terrain was rising in elevation and displaying new types of vegetation, including more grassy meadows and large pine forests. Numerous dry creek beds cut through the forest, making it difficult to maintain a consistent direction of travel. Fortunately, as the afternoon sun moved into the western sky, Li was able to recalibrate his direction and stay on course.

One morning Li finished his coffee and biscuits and decided to find a scenic view for his morning meditation. He met up with one of the creek beds and followed it downstream to see where it led. After a short walk, the creek bed emerged from the pine forest and disappeared into a series of rocky outcrops and ledges. He was left standing on a large boulder that looked out over a most spectacular panorama. From atop the boulder, Li could see for miles in every direction across the flat highland desert. As beautiful as the desert was, mother nature felt compelled to carve a majestic canyon five thousand feet deep into the earth's crust, revealing the colorful rock formations of her past. With the morning sun shining brightly in the crystal blue sky, the graphic story on the canyon wall was clearly illuminated in its fullest glory. The white sandstone rim stood tall at the top of the canyon, giving way to endless layers of history spoken in reds, purples, and pinks leading down into the bottomless depths of time. Li stood on top of the ledge and strained his eyes toward the bottom of the canyon, where he could barely see the river winding proudly through the canyon, just as it had been doing for millions of years.

Li sat down on the rock ledge and revered the grand landscape before him. He found it difficult to grasp the magnitude of such a natural phenomenon and could not find the words to describe his feelings. *Humble* was all he could think of as he gazed out across the majestic canyon and tried to comprehend the scale of time and space of such an epic event. As he sat in awe of nature's creation before him, he was reminded of the words of Tao.

> *Nothing in this world is softer or more gentle than water*
> *Yet nothing can triumph so easily*
> *It is weak, yet it overcomes the strong*
> *It is soft, yet it overcomes the hard*
> *It is yielding, yet none can wear it away*

Li rested in quiet meditation while the morning sun awakened the beautiful canyon below. It was truly a transformative moment, allowing him to step back from his self-centered posture and experience the realities of the natural world as a participant rather than an observer. For the first time in his spiritual practice, he experienced a unique connection to the entirety of the natural world. From this perspective, Li realized how everything was interrelated and fit together in harmonious perfection to form the whole of the natural universe. Just then, he remembered the phrase his grandfather used upon returning home from his spiritual retreats—*"The universe is unfolding exactly as it should"*—and now he understood what his grandfather meant, and it all made perfect sense. After several minutes of quiet solitude, Li returned to camp, prepared his bags, and set out on his journey home with a newfound clarity in his heart.

Li followed the river from atop the canyon for a few more days. Once it began to turn south, Li felt it was time to part ways. He filled all of his canteens with water, made sure Lucky was hydrated and then headed west. The terrain quickly dropped in elevation and the surroundings took on a more desert-like feeling. The days heated up to unbearable temperatures and the nights were cold and dry. Li tried to keep a brisk pace to help get through the desert but was careful not to exhaust himself, or his horse during the peak periods of heat. After a couple of hard and tiring days, Li started to travel more during the early, pre-dawn hours, taking advantage of the cooler temperatures, and resting in the sparse shade during the high heat of the afternoons. This made everything much more comfortable for both Lucky and himself.

Fortunately, after a few more days of rigorous travel, the desert was behind them and replaced with another beautiful mountain range, along with cooler temperatures and tree-covered shade. Li followed a valley westbound through the mountains and over the top of the range. As he traveled down the west side of the mountains, he found himself immersed in a grove of enormous pine trees, unlike anything he had ever seen before. Each of these trees was firmly rooted deep into the ground with a base trunk over twenty feet in diameter and layers of bark over a foot thick. Standing next to one of these massive trees was like standing next to a giant wall. It was hard to imagine something so massive as an actual living species. Li could barely see the sky above him due to the canopy of leaf-covered branches extending outward in every direction and rising several hundred feet skyward. Underneath the giant canopy, numerous smaller trees, shrubs, and flowers thrived in the diffused light and the cool, moist air. Li dismounted and walked slowly through the forest, experiencing the unique network within the forest ecosystem. The giant trees provided a perfectly temperate climate on the forest floor, allowing for a plethora of plants and animals to thrive. The soil was rich and moist, giving life to endless species living comfortably beneath the canopy. Walking through the old-growth forest, Li became awakened by the sensuous energies that filled the air. He was fascinated by the integrated communion of the world in which he found himself. Everything seemed to be in perfect harmony, the way life was meant to be.

Li set camp at the edge of the forest. Following supper, he settled under the comfortable forest canopy and drifted off into a peaceful sleep. He began dreaming about his recent canyon experience. He saw himself standing, once again, on the large boulder overlooking the deep canyon walls towering above the river below. Suddenly, his pulse quickened in anticipation of another dreadful nightmare. He walked closer and closer to the edge, with the dark canyon looming large. From the edge of the canyon, he took the last fatal step off the wall and immediately waved his arms desperately in reaction to the falling sensation. He quickly realized he was not falling at all. Instead, a bright light illuminated from the bottom of the canyon and shined directly on Li's chest. It was this beam of light that suspended Li in mid-air. Li was not falling; he was soaring across the sky in perfect control. As he looked down on the beautiful river winding through the colorful canyon, Li surrendered completely, and fell into the warm embrace of the light, and let it take complete control of his destiny.

Eventually, Li and Lucky made their way to the Pacific Ocean. It was truly a welcome site, indicating an end to the long and arduous journey. As Li approached the outskirts of San Francisco, he came upon a beautiful ranch property framed with log fencing and nestled in a fertile valley overlooking the ocean. There was a small herd of horses grazing in one of the meadows when Li and Lucky rode by.

"How does this place look, Lucky?" Li said as he patted his horse on the neck. "Do you think you could live here?"

Li rode down the path to the main house and stood by the gate until he saw a man come out onto the porch. He was an older man, still fit and active, dressed in jeans and a flannel shirt with suspenders hanging loosely below his waist.

"What can I do for you, neighbor?" the man asked.

"Well, sir. I was hoping you might find a home for my horse."

"I'm not buying any more horses. I'm retired now."

"Oh, I was not trying to sell my horse. You see, we are at the end of a long journey. And I will be boarding a ship to Asia in a few days. I was hoping you might let him live out his last days here on your beautiful ranch."

The man walked down to the gate and took a closer look at Li's horse. "What's your name fella?"

"This is Lucky. And my name is Li."

"How long you been on the trail, Li?"

"About 3 months, I guess. We started in Omaha."

The man looked the horse over thoroughly and then looked at Li. "You know you could sell this horse easily in town."

"Perhaps. But I am more interested in Lucky's wellbeing after I am gone."

"Well, he looks pretty healthy. Does he have any problems getting along with other horses?"

"Not at all, sir."

The man thought a bit more and then opened the gate. "Well, if you're sure you want to give him away, I'll make sure he gets everything he needs from here on out."

"That's wonderful, sir," Li said as he shook the man's hand.

"Put him in one of the stalls in the barn, so he can get used to things."

Li walked up to the barn with Lucky, removed his saddle and led him into a stall. "I think you are going to like it here, Lucky."

There was a moment of sadness in Li's eyes as he said his last goodbye to Lucky. Li transferred all of his gear into his bedroll and gave Lucky one more big hug before closing the stall and walking out of the barn.

"Thanks again, sir," Li said to the man on the porch.

"Good luck, son."

Li walked through the gate and started up the path. He stopped and looked back at the man on the porch.

"Excuse me, sir. What is the name of your ranch?"

"Heaven's Gate," the man replied.

Li smiled at the poetic beauty of the name. Then he waved to the man one final time and walked back up the path.

As Li walked north toward San Francisco, he passed numerous trappers, prospectors, and pioneer families, all seeking a new life in the vast unsettled territories of California. The travelers all seemed so excited and full of energy. They had a wagon full of hopes and dreams, and a blind devotion to succeed. Li could not help but admire these adventurous souls, as they sought out their fame and fortune on the American frontier. Even though many of these crusades would end in failure, every experience seemed to further define the character of the American people and lay the foundation for a strong and resilient culture. As Li thought back through his time in America, he found validation of this belief over and over again. While the lessons of failure helped define the American frontier, it was ultimately the strength of the communities that established a lasting foothold and provided the foundation for stability and success.

CHAPTER THIRTEEN

The captain's horn sounded one last time as the steamship pulled away from the dock. Li stood on the open deck at the ship's stern, looking back at the mainland. He was surprised by the strong emotions he had leaving America. He realized how attached he had become to this country, and especially the people he came to know and love. Despite the negative experiences he encountered, he was left with an abundance of wonderful memories with wonderful people. He admired the virtuous qualities in so many of the people he encountered along the way. Like the enthusiasm in Elliot that was so spirited and contagious. Or the faithfulness that he saw in Shen. Of course, it was the kindness and selfless generosity in Rose that he so loved and admired. And the endless courage and integrity that both Mr. and Mrs. Lincoln displayed time and time again in such difficult circumstances. And then he found the pearls of spiritual strength and leadership in Ouray and his father that reminded him of Panchen and why he admired them all so much. Li recognized that his fundamental Buddhist teachings are manifested everyday throughout the world, doing great things for people everywhere. As Li looked back on his journey, he realized just how much he had learned and grown from his experiences in America. He felt an authentic sense of truth and empowerment from his journey that will remain in his soul forever and, hopefully, give new meaning to his relationship with the people of Tibet. Li watched the coastline disappear into the horizon, and then he walked up to the bow of the boat and began looking forward to his return home.

Pulling into the port at Shanghai caused a bit of anxiety in Li. It had been several years since he had been back to China, and he was unsure exactly what to expect. Also, he had been traveling under a different identity for so long, he felt somewhat foreign and detached from his origins. He decided that it would be best to spend as little time as possible in Shanghai. He was sure that his long hair and simple clothes would sufficiently disguise his true identity, at least until he chose to revert back to his anointed title.

Li exited the ship and proceeded to find a nearby hotel. After checking into his room and washing up for dinner, he walked back out onto the streets to find supplies for his journey home. His first objective was to find a horse stable, where he could hire a team to take him to Tibet. It took a few unsuccessful attempts before he found a stable large enough to put a team together for such a long journey.

"We can support you to Lhasa," the stable owner said. "But you will also be responsible for the cost to return my men and animals to Shanghai."

"I understand, sir. And I will ensure that the team is well supplied and prepared for their return to Shanghai."

"Good. I will need a few days to get everything in order," the man said. "How do you plan to pay for this?"

"Well, sir, I can pay for a portion of the cost now and will pay the balance from my accounts in Lhasa, when we arrive."

"This is no small sum, you understand," the man stated, somewhat doubtful of Li's financial abilities.

"I understand. And I can assure you that everything will be settled once we reach Potala palace."

"Potala palace? Do you have accounts at Potala palace? How is that possible? You look like a commoner to me."

"Yes, well, I have just returned from America, and have not yet had an opportunity to clean up sufficiently." Sensing the man's increasing skepticism, Li reached into his bag and displayed a handful of solid gold coins. "I have ten gold coins that I will give you today, and I will pay the balance in gold coins when we arrive in Lhasa."

The stable owner took one of the coins from Li's hand and inspected it closely. "Come back in three days and everything will be ready to go," the owner said as he reached out and removed the remaining coins from the open hand.

Li smiled and shook the man's hand. "Thank you, sir.

I will be back on Thursday morning."

Li was closing the gate when the owner hollered back to Li, "What is your name, young man?"

Li started to reply but paused and became speechless for a moment. "Gyatso," he finally replied.

"See you on Thursday, Gyatso," the owner said.

Over the next few days, the word spread around town that a monk from the Potala palace was commissioning a small team to support him on his journey back to Lhasa. When Gyatso returned to the stables on Thursday morning, several interested parties were waiting for him. First, was the team that had been hired to escort Gyatso on the trip. This team was handpicked by the owner and consisted of the best Buddhist Sherpas available in Shanghai.

"Mister Gyatso," the owner began. "I would like to introduce you to your team of Sherpas."

Gyatso bowed and shook hands with each Sherpa as he was introduced. "Thank you all for your commitment to making this trip. I look forward to your experienced guidance, as well as your friendly companionship."

The second group of interest came from some local Buddhist residents who had heard about the traveling monk. It was never confirmed exactly who the monk was, or just how important he was in the Buddhist monastery, but the few devout Buddhists that had assembled were most grateful when Gyatso greeted each of the followers with a bow and a personal blessing.

The last group of interest came from the Senior Ambassador and a few representatives from the Qing administration. Gyatso recognized the Ambassador from the last Leadership Summit.

"Good morning Mister Gyatso," the Ambassador said as he shook hands and looked closely, trying to identify Gyatso. "I do not believe we have met. I am Mister Zhao, a Senior Ambassador with the Qing commission."

Concerned that the ambassador might recognize him and create an uncomfortable situation, Gyatso replied, "Good morning Mister Ambassador. It is so thoughtful of you to take the time to welcome me to your city. Perhaps we can take a short walk together." Gyatso pointed to a path leading down to the pasture.

The two men walked down to the field and stopped next to a corral of horses feeding in the pasture nearby.

"We have known about the Dalai Lama missing from the Potala palace for a long time," the Ambassador stated.

"Yes, I expect that you have. I hope that you will keep my identity to yourself, at least until I have departed. I would prefer that my support team not know of my true identity while we are traveling together."

"I'm afraid that everyone is already aware of your identity, Your Holiness."

Gyatso turned and looked back up the path at the growing number of people gathered near the stables. "I see. Well then, I guess I have no choice but to accept the circumstances and make the most of my journey home."

"If I may ask a question, Your Holiness," the Ambassador said.

"Of course."

"Now that you have traveled to America, what have you learned and what are your intentions for Tibet now?"

The Dalai Lama had obviously thought about this question numerous times over the last several months. However, he was surprised that the question had been asked so soon upon his return to Asia.

"Mister Ambassador, my trip to America has taught me that change is inevitable, and we cannot always control our future. What we can control is how we react to those changes that impact our lives. This is not a new discovery to me or to the people of Tibet. We have always been taught to never fight with fate and to do what it means to be an ethical person beyond hope and fear. With regard to my intentions going forward, I plan to align Tibet with any country that recognizes our independence and shares our reverence for the history, culture, and natural beauty so unique to Tibet and its people."

"Thank you, Your Holiness," replied the Ambassador. "You have made your intentions quite clear. However, the Qing administration is concerned for Tibet's safety, given the recent advances in Asia by European interests. I would propose that you delay your trip for a day or two so that you can meet with our foreign minister. I am certain he could provide valuable insights regarding this matter."

His Holiness turned back toward the stables as he

replied, "Apparently, I have not made my intentions clear enough. Unless things have changed while I was away, your Empire does not recognize Tibet's sovereignty and has no interest in the preservation of our country's history, culture, or natural resources. However, I will express your concerns to the High Lamas when I return to Lhasa. Now, if you will please excuse me, I must begin my journey back home."

The two men walked back up to the stables, where the Sherpas were packed and ready for departure. The Dalai Lama thanked the stable owner once again for his assistance in preparing for this journey on such short notice. He then turned and bowed graciously to the crowd of devoted Buddhists, which had now grown to an extraordinary number of followers. The Dalai Lama mounted his horse and fell in line with the team as they followed the narrow trail down to the Yangtze River.

Suddenly, the Sherpa team stopped after they heard a loud commotion coming from the horse stables back up the hill. There was screaming and yelling in the crowd as several uniformed men on horseback tried to ride through the crowd. As the government marshals became more aggressive with the civilians, the yelling became louder and more desperate. Just then, the gate to the trail swung open and the crowd swarmed down the hill and began sitting on the trail and locking arms with one another. In a matter of seconds, there was a human barrier assembled across the trail and down the hill. The Qing marshals tried to ride through the massive barrier, but the horses would not advance into the entangled bodies of the protesters. The Sherpa team quickly reacted to the chaos by splitting up. One group surrounded the Dalai Lama and continuing down the trail at an accelerated pace, while the second group of Sherpas dismounted and prepared to defend the trail behind them. When the Dalai Lama and his Sherpa team disappeared into the river valley, the Ambassador called off the marshals and the chaos subsided.

The trip across the rugged mountains of South China was long and hard. It seemed like it took forever to finally crest the last mountain pass and see the city of Lhasa nestled in the valley below. Seeing Lhasa made the Dalai Lama's heart race with nervous excitement. He had thought about his return ever since he boarded the ship back in San Francisco. It had been years since he had left home. He was uncertain exactly how the palace had reacted to his departure, and even more uncertain how they would react to his return after so long. He was not the same person who left, and he expected that would be immediately evident to the people closest to him. Regardless, he knew that he would be welcomed home and his anxiety was purely self-induced.

On the night before they were to arrive in the city, the Dalai Lama shaved all of the hair off his face and head. He had become quite accustomed to having hair on his head, and perhaps he would grow it out again someday. But for now, he needed to be uniform and recognizable.

The Dalai Lama instructed one of the Sherpas to ride into the Potala palace and notify the monastery of his arrival.

"Ask for Panchen Lama only," he instructed the Sherpa. "Do not tell anyone else about my arrival. And instruct Panchen Lama to meet me at the stables alone."

It was dark when the Dalai Lama reached Lhasa. He managed to guide the Sherpas around the town center and up to the Potala palace without anyone noticing his arrival. As he rode through the gates of the palace stables, he saw Panchen standing alone near the office. The Dalai Lama dismounted and walked swiftly toward his mentor and friend and collapsed into his arms. Their long embrace allowed the years of pent-up emotions to pour out of them both.

"Your Holiness," Panchen said as he wiped his tears. "I do not have the words to express my feelings at this moment."

"I understand, Panchen. This must be an enormous surprise. I did not want to make my arrival known, as I knew I would be tired and in need of some rest before greeting everyone else."

Both men wiped their tears again and laughed at their display of emotional weakness.

"Yes, of course," Panchen replied. "You must be exhausted. Please, go and get some rest. I will find rooms for the Sherpas and see that the animals are cared for."

"Thank you, Panchen. We have a lot to talk about and I look forward to your updates."

The men hugged once more and then Gyatso proceeded to his quarters for a long and welcome rest.

The Dalai Lama had been sleeping for two days when he was awakened by something making a noise at the window. He sat up in bed and listened closely, and then realized exactly what it was. He immediately rose and opened the window.

"Lobsang," he whispered. "How did you know I was home?"

"You've been asleep for two days. Everyone knows your home by now."

"I'm awake now. Come up and see me."

Lobsang climbed up the lattice to the open deck and then through the window. "Gyatso, my good friend. It is so good to see you," he said as he gave his friend a big hug.

"Oh, Lobsang, I think I missed you more than anyone."

"So, tell me. Is America everything we imagined?'

"Yes, and more."

"Oh, I knew it! I cannot wait to hear about every little detail."

"Yes, we have a lot to talk about. How about you, my friend? Are you well?"

"Yes, I am most well and happy," Lobsang said with a broad smile. "I have some big news myself."

"Wait, let me guess. You completed your Buddhist

monk training and are now an ordained monk."

Lobsang laughed nervously. "Actually, quite the opposite. You see, I met a girl and fell in love," Lobsang paused for a moment, trying to contain his excitement. "We are now married and expecting our first child in a few months."

"Lobsang! I cannot believe my ears."

"I know it is not what you expected. But I do hope that you are happy for me."

The thought of Lobsang in love took Gyatso back to his time with Rose. Though he could not tell Lobsang about the love of his life, he understood exactly how Lobsang felt.

"My dear friend. I am overwhelmed with joy for you. You have chosen a path that will bring endless moments of happiness and gratitude. I have no doubt you made the right choice, and you will be a wonderful husband and father."

"Thank you, Gyatso. I was nervous about telling you. But I can see the happiness in your eyes, and I am most grateful to receive your blessing."

The two men smiled and hugged again.

"So, I have been sleeping for two days?"

"Yes, you have. And I am told the High Lamas are anxious to meet with you."

"Yes, well, I certainly owe them an explanation," he said with a guilty smile.

"I better go and let you rest. I am so glad you are home, and I cannot wait for you to meet my wife Pema."

"It's good to see you, my friend. We will get together soon, I promise."

Lobsang crawled through the window and onto the deck. He then turned and stuck his head back into Gyatso's room.

"Just so you know," Lobsang said. "Not everyone was in support of your trip to America. Many of the Tibetan people felt abandoned when you disappeared for so long. It was Panchen that kept the sangha together. He was your biggest advocate and supporter all this time."

The Dalai Lama closed the window behind Lobsang and watched as he disappeared into the darkness. He crawled back into bed and tried to sleep. His mind was racing with thoughts and he quickly realized the futility of his effort. Besides, he decided that he was starving. So, he got dressed and proceeded down to the kitchen to find some hot tea and breakfast.

When the Dalai Lama reached the kitchen, he found the lights were already on and the kitchen staff enjoying breakfast before starting their daily routines. When they saw His Holiness enter the room, they all stood and bowed politely.

"Good morning, everyone," His Holiness began. "Please, sit down and enjoy your breakfast. I can serve myself today."

The kitchen manager nodded to the staff to sit down and continue eating breakfast. "We heard that you were home, Your Holiness. We are all grateful for your safe return and especially happy to see you this day."

"Thank you, my dear. It is great to be back home," he said as he poured himself a cup of tea and a bowl of hot porridge. "May I sit with you all this morning? I would feel lost and lonely sitting in the dining room all by myself."

"Of course, Your Holiness. We would be honored," the manager replied.

The Dalai Lama sat down at the kitchen table with the staff and engaged in a casual and most enjoyable conversation. He told them stories of his journey and the staff related events that he had missed while he was away.

"It is so nice to have a good cup of tea. You cannot find tea easily in America. The Americans all drink coffee. Have you ever tried coffee?"

The manager looked around the table. "I do not think so."

"Well, it's color is black as night and the taste is even stronger than it looks."

The staff all looked at each other and giggled.

"And some people will add cow's milk to their coffee."

The giggles got louder.

"Oh, and the elegant people will hold their cup like this," he said as he lifted his cup in the air and extended his little finger straight out from the cup.

Finally, the giggles turned into full laughter by the entire table.

About that time, Panchen walked into the kitchen.

"My goodness," he said with a smile. "It sounds like a

festival in here." As he scanned the table, he quickly noticed His Holiness sitting alongside everyone else, having breakfast. "Your Holiness, I didn't expect to see you in here."

"Yes, well, after two days of sleeping, I discovered I was starving. So, I came down for an early breakfast."

"I see. Perhaps you would like to join me in the dining room?"

"Of course," His Holiness said as he stood up. "Thank you all for a most enjoyable breakfast," he said to the staff. "I hope we can do this again soon."

The staff all stood up with broad smiles and bowed to the Dalai Lama as he and Panchen exited the kitchen.

"I was wondering when you might wake up from your slumber," Panchen said as he sat down in the dining hall.

"Yes, well, I cannot believe how long I was asleep. My body must have been completely drained. I feel great now."

"That's good. Some people have been waiting to see you," Panchen said as he pointed to the window.

The Dalai Lama walked to the south windows overlooking the amphitheater. To his surprise, the amphitheater was completely packed with people sitting in every corner of the facility. Not only that, he could also see the long winding path leading down the hillside into Lhasa was packed with loyal followers as well.

"My goodness, Panchen. I am overwhelmed by this response."

"Well, word spread rather quickly of your return. Many of these people have been out there since you arrived."

The Dalai Lama stood at the window, in complete awe of what he was seeing. He had worried often about how the community would receive him, but never did he expect such a display of compassion and loyalty. With joyful tears in his eyes, he felt his heart swell with love and happiness.

After Panchen had been served his breakfast, Gyatso sat alongside him while he ate.

"Panchen, I want to apologize to you for the way I abandoned you in Shanghai. I realize now it was a selfish gesture by me, and I am truly sorry for leaving you alone with such a burden."

"It was a long ride back to Lhasa," Panchen replied. "I will say that much for sure."

"Well, I was told that you have been a noble steward of the sangha, and you continued to advocate for me even during times of doubt."

"Your Holiness, since the day I first lifted you from the crib, I have known that you were special. You have the gift of curiosity, which has led you to discover attributes in yourself and others that no one else realized. You have always interpreted the Buddhist tenets in a way that made everyone think differently and ultimately strengthened their beliefs as well as yours. So, when you got on that ship to America, I was terrified. There were times when I never expected to see you again. But during times of quiet reflection, I felt your presence, and I knew that you were safe. I believed in you and I trusted that you would return home with newfound discoveries and knowledge."

"You were right to be terrified," Gyatso said. "But you were also right to believe in me. My behavior may have been selfish, but my intentions never were. I was always seeking the truth, both within myself and in the cultural conflicts we see emerging in this world."

"Yes, we continue to struggle with this threat," Panchen stated.

"But that may be our problem, Panchen. We are trying to find a solution that lies completely outside our realm of thought."

"I'm afraid I don't understand."

"The Tibetans have spent endless lifetimes eradicating greed and fear from our consciousness. How could we ever use those same weapons now to defend ourselves? If we are to survive, we must play to our strengths, now more than ever. This is about the manifestation of peace and happiness inside every human heart. It should be truth that serves as our fortress, with knowledge and compassion as our greatest weapons."

"Perhaps you are right," Panchen said. "But we are just a small country, isolated from the rest of the world."

"That is true. But our spiritual foundation links us to millions of Buddha warriors carrying the same truths and insights. If we include the whole of the Buddhist world, our voices will be loud and strong. A single twig is soon broken and discarded, but a bundle of twigs, held together, withstands all forces."

"This is a lot to process, Your Holiness. Perhaps we should continue this conversation later with the High Lamas."

"Of course, Panchen," the Dalai Lama said as he stood and placed his hand on Panchen's shoulder. "In the meantime, I am reminded of one of your favorite Buddha quotes. *'Contentment is our greatest wealth.'* Now, if you will excuse me, I think I will go meet some friends."

Panchen stood up and walked to the window overlooking the amphitheater. He could hear the thunderous screams and cheers as the Dalai Lama walked out onto the stage. He watched the massive crowd drop to their knees in collective reverence to their beloved leader. Panchen realized the beautiful child that he lifted from the cradle so many years ago was now a grown man, complete with the knowledge and understanding of what it means to be enlightened with Buddha nature.

Standing on the stage in front of his loyal congregation filled the Dalai Lama with unbridled joy. It had been years since he wore the banner of a spiritual leader. It, somehow, seemed different this time. He felt less anxiety, for sure. But there was something else inside his heart that made him feel safer and more comfortable. It was as if he held the trust of every soul in the amphitheater, and now he knew exactly what to do with that trust.

Instead of speaking to the congregation on this day,

the Dalai Lama felt compelled to engage with his faithful followers in a more intimate way. He proceeded to walk down the steps of the stage into the crowded amphitheater. As he walked past his brothers and sisters, they all stood and greeted him with joy and praise. He walked slowly through the crowd, shaking hands, hugging children, and acknowledging everyone he could as he walked by. When he had reached the top of the crowded amphitheater, he looked down at the endless stream of followers assembled on the road into town. With humility and a full heart, the Dalai Lama proceeded down the crowded road, blessing every soul he could reach while being blessed by all the grace and strength they bestowed upon him.

ABOUT ATMOSPHERE PRESS

Atmosphere Press is an independent, full-service publisher for excellent books in all genres and for all audiences. Learn more about what we do at atmospherepress.com.

We encourage you to check out some of Atmosphere's latest releases, which are available at Amazon.com and via order from your local bookstore:

This Side of Babylon, a novel by James Stoia

Within the Gray, a novel by Jenna Ashlyn

Where No Man Pursueth, a novel by Micheal E. Jimerson

Here's Waldo, a novel by Nick Olson

Tales of Little Egypt, a historical novel by James Gilbert

For a Better Life, a novel by Julia Reid Galosy

The Hidden Life, a novel by Robert Castle

Big Beasts, a novel by Patrick Scott

Alvarado, a novel by John W. Horton III

Nothing to Get Nostalgic About, a novel by Eddie Brophy

GROW: A Jack and Lake Creek Book, a novel by Chris S McGee

Home is Not This Body, a novel by Karahn Washington

Whose Mary Kate, a novel by Jane Leclere Doyle

Stuck and Drunk in Shadyside, a novel by M. Byerly

These Things Happen, a novel by Chris Caldwell

ABOUT THE AUTHOR

Marcus Wiley grew up on the Front Range of Colorado. It was through exploring the Rocky Mountains that his passion for nature and the history of the American West was intimately instilled. He also spent much of his adult life working in foreign countries, where his interest in Asian cultures and philosophies emerged. With these memories as his backdrop, Marcus spent several years creating this fictional story that reflects the beauty and insights of his collective past.

Find out more at www.MJWiley.com

CPSIA information can be obtained
at www.ICGtesting.com
Printed in the USA
LVHW030435080321
680820LV00023B/587

9 781636 495705